Printed
For
Quixote Press
by
BRENNAN PRINTING
100 Main Street
Deep River, Iowa 52222
515-595-2000

Gun Shootin', Girl Chasin', Whiskey Drinkin'
Tales out of The Land of the Lakes

by

Netha Bell

QUIXOTE PRESS
R.R. #4, Box 33B
Blvd. Station
Sioux City, Iowa 51109

* * * * * * * * * *

**QUIXOTE
PRESS**
Bruce Carlson
R.R. #4, Box 33B
Blvd. Station
Sioux City, Iowa
51109

PRINTED
IN
U.S.A.

Acknowledgements

I wish to acknowledge the encouragement all my family and friends have given me in my writing!!

DEDICATION

I wish to dedicate this book to my long time friend, Millie McKinney of Frederic, Wisconsin who has enthusiastically supported me in my writing.

The reader must appreciate the fact that some of these stories could prove to be embarrassing to some folks today. Because of that, some of these stories use fictitious names. In those cases, it should be understood that any similarity between those names and actual persons, living or dead, is purely coincidental.

PREFACE

This is a collection of tales from the heart of the Midwest lake country and north woods.

These tales tell us of what life (and death) was like when the land was rough and folks wrestled a living from it.

FOREWORD

Netha Bell has poked around the lake shores and woods of the northern Midwest and found some stories about all kinds of stuff for this book GUN SHOOTIN', GIRL CHASIN', WHISKEY DRINKIN' TALES OUT of the LAND OF THE LAKES.

- Prof Phil Hey
Briar Cliff College
Sioux City, Iowa

TABLE OF CONTENTS

CHAPTER ONE

LOGGERS TURNED FARMERS

lack River Falls is in Jackson County in western Wisconsin. It lies on the western bank of the Black River. Once, in its hey-day many years ago, logs tumbled over these high falls. One of Wisconsin's first sawmills was built there. Now, a power dam has curbed the flow of the water. Just below the bridge, the channel is heaped with slabs and blocks of quartzite.

Black River Falls, when it was young, was a brawling lumber town. The loggers came into town on payday and celebrated with lots of gusto!

On one particular Saturday night, about 40 loggers were celebrating in their usual style — guzzling whiskey, brawling, and raisin' cain.

"Hey, ya old wood-chippers!" Henry Dowds called

out at the top of his lungs, being well into his cups.
"Let's have us sum fun whet say?"

"Whet ya got in
mine, Henry?" Turk
Lowrey asked.

"Don't know, yet.
But let's git outa
here an' go lookin',"
Henry replied.

"Sokay by me,"
Turk remarked.
"Are ya all with
us?" he asked the
other loggers.

Looking at each other, they all nodded in agreement. There was a mass exodus of the "Rot-Gut
Saloon" as the loggers swayed and staggered out
the door.

As Bart Thurman and Andy Potts watched the
drunken loggers leave, Bart turned to Andy and
said, "Think we might otter keep an eye on 'em?"

"Hell, man, we're way outnumbered!" Bart replied.

"Yaw, but ta see what they might be up to, that's
all."

So, the two local citizens trailed at a safe distance.
They saw the group of men headed toward the
blacksmith shop and stop. There was lots of

laughing and yelling and a good deal of swearing.

Shortly, out
through the
door burst
several of
the loggers
pulling a
breaking
plow by a
heavy rope.
Gripping the
handles to
guide it was
Henry
Dowds.

"Gee, haw, ya old wood-chippers!" yelled Henry.
"Git yer rears ta goin'! We 'uns got some plowin'
ta do 'fore mornin'!"

The loggers started out at the front of the
blacksmith shop. There were about a dozen men
pulling the rope while old Henry tried to guide it.
Taking turns, they worked back and forth, plowing
up about two blocks of the dirt street. It was hard
work, but they seemed to figure it was worth it.

Working the better part of the night, the rowdy
gang finally had made a plowed field out of the
main street of town. After finishing their chore,
they put the plow back into the smithy's shop.

"Whet we gonna do now, Henry?" Turk asked,
"Ah'm tard!"

"Aw, hell, Turk, we're a fair piece frum bein' done!
We got us some plantin' ta do!" Henry told him.

The loggers followed Henry up to the feed store.
Henry tried the doorknob, but of course found it
locked.

"How they 'spect to do business if they's gonna
close up suh early?" Henry asked. "Ah need a rock,
somebody, anybody. Git me a rock so's Ah kin get
this here door opened!"

"Henry! Do ya really think
we orter?" Turk asked.

"Why, shore! We'uns gotta
git our crops planted, don't
we?"

Someone handed Henry a
rock. He broke out the pane
of glass, reached inside and
unlocked the door. Some of
the men followed Henry inside. The others stayed outside the store and waited.
Bart and Andy, the local men, watched from across
the street.

Pretty soon the loggers came out, each carrying
a sack on his shoulder. Then they stacked the sacks
in a pile. Henry opened the first one.

"Okay, men. Each of ya git some of these here
seeds and let's start plantin'!"

The loggers walked up an down the furrowed street, throwing the seed this way and that.

Black River Falls, not having a marshal to keep law and order, was at the mercy of these rowdy, drunken loggers.

Finally, Bart Thurman could stand it no longer. He crossed the street to where Henry Dowds was scattering seed.

"What in tarnation are ya men a-doin'?" Bart asked.

"Doin'? Doin'? Don'tcha know whet we's a-doin'? Why we're sowin' our wild oats, thet's what!!" Henry roared!

CHAPTER TWO

THE DUEL

ack in the early 1900's, in Polk County in northwestern Minnesota, lived two old bachelor brothers, Frank and Gordy Thomas. They had inherited a small farm when their parents passed on. They had one sister, Kate, who wanted nothing more to do with either the farm or her brothers after she moved to St. Paul. Frank and Gordy referred to her as "Miss Hoity-Toity"!

The pair of brothers weren't necessarily bachelors by choice. They both liked the fairer sex. The plain truth was, they were not a very good catch — either one of them! Both were lazy, to the point of being shiftless. And their personal habits didn't exactly draw girls like flies.

The two men did take a bath every month of two, whether they needed it or not. Frank always wore his long-handled underwear, even in the summertime, because it was too much of an effort to change out of them.

Gordy, on the other hand, did change every once in a while - underpants, that is, not his overalls. That denim article of clothing, should one have been able to get him to part with them, would have stood alone in a corner.

Although their father was quite a hunter in his day, he hadn't passed the skill on to his sons. If they had to rely on their hunting ability for their meat, they would have starved to death. Their diet consisted of the eggs that their few hens laid and some puny vegetables they half-heartedly raised. Occasionally the "boys" would buy a little meat from a neighbor or at the grocery store in town. They also ate a lot of rice, and some fish - if they felt energetic enough to go fishing, that is!

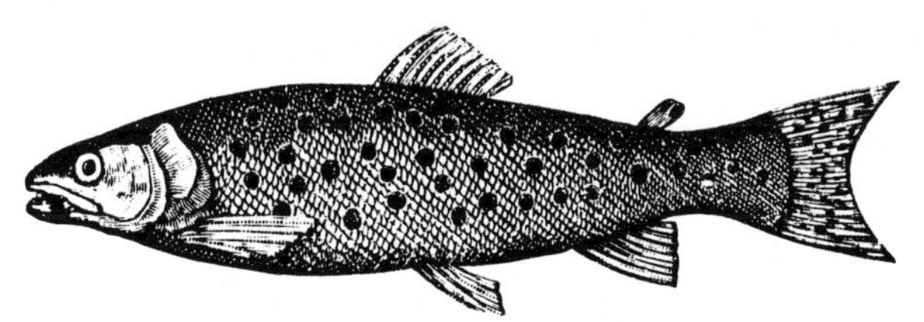

One day late in summer, the brothers happened to be in town when Miss Louella Daviess came into their lives. She was the new school marm and as pretty as a speckled pup. They watched as the Reverend Barnes helped Miss Louella down from the buckboard. He then carried her baggage into Miss Carrie's, who took in boarders.

Frank and Gordy were sitting on an old splintered bench in front of the "Durndefino Saloon". They'd bought a jug of rot-gut earlier and were sharing it. The other patrons of the saloon were glad about the two old bachelors' choice of seats. They smelled too gamey to share a table with.

"Well," Frank ventured. "Do you see what I see, Gordy?" he inquired of his brother. "That's a mighty purty little filly 'cross the way!"

"Yup," Gordy slurred, "but I'll jist betcha ain't stallion 'nuff ta go over and say 'hi', are ya?"

Frank made a feeble ef- fort to stand up, but he'd had too many swigs out of the jug to make the grade.

"Well, now, I'll jist betcha two-bits that you cain't neither," Frank said.

"Betcha," Gordy replied, getting to his feet. But as he tried to take a step, he lost his balance and sat back down — kerthud — right on a big splinter!!

"YOWEE, DAMN!!" he yelled, pulling out the splinter.

Miss Louella briefly glanced over her shoulder at the pair, raising one neat little eyebrow, then pointed her nose slightly upward in disgust. Frank and Gordy watched as she entered Miss Carrie's and closed the door behind her.

"Ya lose, Gordy," Frank informed his brother. "Ya owe me two-bits."

The two old bachelors, with lots of staggering and weaving, finally made it to where Petunia, their faithful old nag, was hitched to the wagon. Frank was barely able to get up to the seat. Gordy decided to ride in the wagon bed where he could lie down, as the splinter had hurt his pride.

God only knows how the drunken pair made it home. They probably wouldn't have if Petunia hadn't know the way.

The next day, after waking up with king-sized hangovers, the brothers were both quite testy. They didn't feel much like eating, but were having a cup of strong, black coffee on the front porch, watching their prized young rooster chasing the aged hens.

"Shore wish I had as much energy as thet durned rooster!" Frank remarked. "If I did, would be easy ta git that young filly ta look my way."

"Oh, horsefeathers, Frank! You'd be like one of them there dogs thet chase them newfangled cars. Ya wouldn't know what ta do with it if ya caught it!"

"Oh, the hell ya beller!" Frank retorted. "I jist might s'prize ya!"

"S'prize me? I'd die a-laughin' at ya makin' a fool outer yurself!"

"And I s'pose ya think ya could do better, huh, Gordy? Do ya?" Frank yelled, making his head hurt.

"Shore, if I jist got tha chance," Gordy teased.

The brothers cussed and discussed the situation for quite some time, sharing the jug they'd brought home with them. Frank, the older of the two, thought Gordy was making fun of his age. His face was steadily getting redder, and not from the effects of the booze.

"I'll tell ya what, Gordy Thomas! There's jist one way of settlin' this. A duel!! Who ever comes out tha winner, gits ta go inta town and start courtin' that little filly!" Frank loudly suggested.

"Frank! Have ya completely lost what little mind ya got left in yer fat head? A duel? Thet's the dumbest thing I've ever heerd tell of!"

"Ya heerd me right - a duel! Are ya man 'nuff or are ya too skeered?"

"Skeered? Of you? 'Course I ain't skeered of you. But ya gotta be sittin' on yer brains ta come up with a half-baked idea like thet!"

"Well, now, if ya don't have tha guts ta square off with me in a duel, we'll jist call me tha winner! How's that? Then I'd jist go callin' on thet purty little filly and you'd be outten tha cold."

"Ya danged old fool! She prob'ly wouldn't even give ya tha time a day. But if yer so hell-bent on a duel, I'll jist take ya up on it."

The two old bachelors stumbled into the house and dug around until they found their father's pistols. They did know enough about firearms to make sure the guns were loaded. Then they went back outside.

"Now, then," Frank said. "We walk off in opposite directions. You go towards the chicken yard and I'll go towards thet big old tree. At the count of ten, we turn and fire. Have ya got thet?"

"Yah, I got thet!"

The brothers started walking and counting, each in the opposite direction. They veered slightly, due to the effects of the jug they had sampled.

At the count of ten, both men turned around and fired. But being the "expert marksmen" that they were, neither brother was hurt directly by the bullets. Gordy's hit a low-hanging limb, which, in turn, came down and whumped Frank in the head. This knocked him out colder than a well-digger's

behind!! Frank's bullet went wild and hit the prized rooster just as he was about to catch a hen. The
rooster squawked, jumped in the air, thought 'Boy!
them new white rock hens are sure sumthin-else;'
and gave up the ghost.

Gordy came out of the ruckus unhurt. Frank nurs-
ed a goose-egg on his head for several days. And
as for Miss Louella Daviess, she never knew that
she'd been the object of a duel - such as it was!
Nor did she know that the prized rooster had laid
down his life for her!

CHAPTER THREE

'TIL DEATH (OR WHATEVER)
DO US PART

ne of the lesser known, but most vicious outlaws of the late 1800's was born in Wisconsin. Arthur Louis Stevens came into this world in 1875 at Pittsville. Shortly thereafter, his family moved to Cumberland - one of a quartet of bad-towns at that time. Then in 1889, the family moved to Monong, Wisconsin. Arthur's father deserted his family here. Later, his mother remarried.

The first job that Arthur had was with the railroad. This didn't last too long after he hit a car tapper over the head with a coupling pin.

Next, he was involved in a barroom brawl. This got him into serious trouble with the law. He had killed a man with his bare fists. Arthur got out of the murder charge by pleading self-defense.

About this time, he felt it might be better to leave Wisconsin for Chicago. He dropped his last name and became known as Arthur Louis thereafter.

In Chicago, Arthur met a sweet young thing by the name of Patricia Snowden. They swore their love for each other, and Patricia did remain faithful to him until his death. The young swain decided he could make a fortune for his lady-love if he headed west.

Arthur found out shortly that he didn't have what it took to make it in the raw country. He tried his hand at prospecting but it was too hard a work for what he got out of it. But he had promised Patricia to bring back riches!

In 1895, Arthur became a cowhand and a dead-shot, almost overnight. He went to work on a large ranch near Billings. He was willing to learn and tackled any job he was asked to do. Arthur even had a way of taming wild horses, who became docile at his touch.

With practice, he became a marksman with both a rifle and a six-shooter.

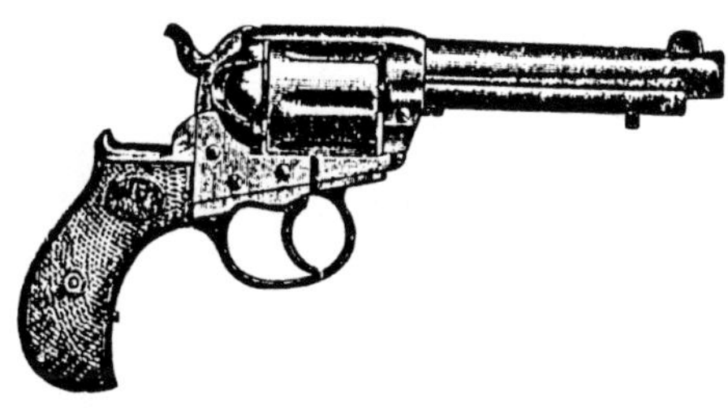

But Arthur was impatient to become rich and return to Patricia. Therefore, he started frequenting the gambling rooms. Here he met Percy Burson - another cowboy. Burson told Louis how he could get some money fast - by rustling! Burson suggesting that they try some of this "moonlighting" and Louis agreed.

During this period of time, Billings, known as the "Hole in the Wall" territory, was run by an outlaw gang called the Red Sash.

"The Red Sash Gang will be blamed for every cow we steal," Burson told Louis.

Within ten days time, working with Burson, Arthur rustled several hundred head of cattle. These brought a good price, and Arthur Louis wanted to get back to Patricia.

"I thoughtcha wanted ta git rich. Really rich, I mean," Burson said. "If we jist do this fer a while, we kin."

The next time at the gambling hall Arthur decided to go along with Burson since he had lost all his money!

The pair of rustlers didn't fare so well on their second try at it. Authorities had suspected Burson of being a cattle thief. Therefore, his plan failed because of the trap the sheriff set. But the big-footed posse alerted the moonlighters by their noise. Burson and Louis fled with the sheriff in hot pursuit.

The men separated, with Burson doubling back toward Billings. But the sheriff and part of the posse were waiting and took Burson without a fight.

The rest of the posse followed Louis into a canyon in the upper Missouri River basin. But knowing that this was a natural fortress, and knowing Louis' skill with a gun, they moved cautiously. One deputy accidentally exposed his arm and Louis put a bullet through it from his hiding place. Then came the Mexican stand-off, each side waiting for the other to make a move.

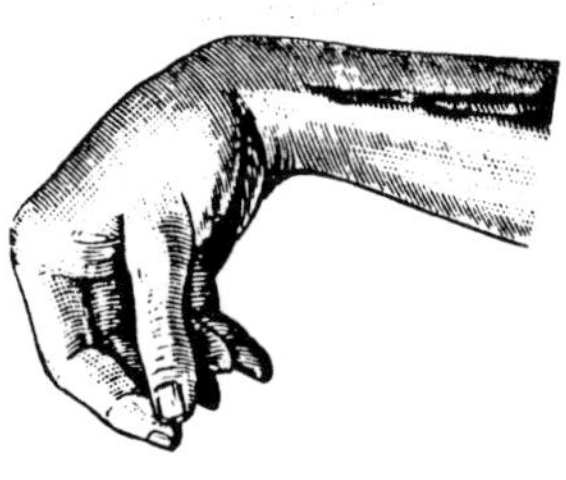

A few minutes before midnight, Louis heard some rocks and pebbles rolling down the side of the canyon. When he fired a shot, he heard a body roll down the mountainside. Immediately, there was the sound of the other deputies scrambling for cover!

Arthur Louis waited for about an hour before he took off his boots and slipped down the hillside. Going into the posse's camp, he picked out the best horse and set the rest of them loose. Louis shot several times in the direction of his enemy's camp and then rode off into the night.

Since he was a branded man anyway, Louis went wildly from one crime to another. He trusted no one after Burson and was a loner. He lived by the motto of "Every man for himself!"

Louis landed in the still untamed city of Seattle in 1898. Here he met Don Merritt, a petty thief who had escaped from the California penitentiary. This friendship ended in tragedy for everyone concerned.

The first job they pulled was holding up a drunk and slugging his companion over the head with a gun. They stole $500. But the police were hot on their heels, so the pair headed toward the Badlands of South Dakota.

This duo had planned to steal the miners' gold at Cripple Creek. But Louis ran into a former acquaintance from the Billings' ranch. This man told him a deputy from Montana was in the area. Merritt thought they should leave right away. Not so, Arthur Louis. He suggested they stay and take their chances. He thought they should hold up the two old prospectors' mine. And so they waited, with masks in place, on the trail leading to the mine.

Imagine their surprise when several miners emerged from the tunnel! But Louis felt cocky enough to take on the whole bunch!

It wasn't as tough as Merritt had thought it would be. When the pair of thieves yelled to the miners to "throw up your hands", they obeyed. Of course, staring down the muzzles of Merritt's and Louis' guns might have had something to do with it!

Talk about guts! The pair then returned to Cripple Creek and sat in a saloon, getting a kick out of hearing others talk about the hold-up and how the thieves had netted over $5,000 in gold dust!

The next morning, the pair boarded a train for Denver. Louis wanted to go see Patricia. But as usual, gambling proved to be his downfall. Within a week, these two-bit thieves were again broke. Out of sheer necessity, they held up a Denver saloon. The customers were locked in a freezer at the rear of the place after Louis and Merritt had relieved them of $500. Fortunately for the poor people, a man walked into the saloon shortly and released them before they died of the cold.

The duo of relentless thievery figured by now that
the Seattle authorities had forgotten about the rob-
bery of the drunk. So, they again boarded the train,
but this time headed for Seattle. During a number
of weeks, they committed several burglaries. But
they gambled away all their "hard earned money".

Then in January of 1899, Don Merritt invited his
friend, Arthur Louis, to visit his home in Portland,
Oregon, where his mother and sister, Mary, lived.

Mary, foolish girl that she was, fell in love with her brother's friend. The two were married shortly.

WELL — SO MUCH FOR UNDYING LOVE!!

CHAPTER FOUR

THE SAWDUST TRAIL

ack around the turn of the century, near Concord, Minnesota, lived one of the area's most eligible bachelors. Clell Tomason was a handsome devil that made many a little girl's heart do double-time. He half-heartedly courted a few, but he was so shy and tongue-tied that they usually lost interest in a short time.

Clell owned a nice little cabin with a big front porch at the edge of town and worked in the logging camp a few miles away. On Sundays, he often had company of the female variety. But Clell didn't appear to take these visitors seriously due to his shyness. And the ladies usually never returned.

In order to cover up this shyness, he turned to being a prankster. Clell had rigged up an outrageous practical joke in his outhouse. There was an overhead toilet tank complete with downpipe and

chain. Those who
had visited this "lit-
tle house outback"
knew the toilet tank
was far from nor-
mal. When they
pulled the chain, a
bolt was released
that let two hinged
parts of the bottom
to come open. But
it wasn't water that
showered the un-
suspecting visitor.
No!! It was a pail
full of clean sawdust
Clell had brought
home from the logging camp. This little trick had
discouraged and cooled the ardor of many an
otherwise enthused cutie.

One very warm Sunday afternoon in July, Mr. and
Mrs. August Olson, good friends of Clell's who lived
at the north
edge of town,
came visiting.
They brought
along Miss
Betsy Callahan,
their niece who
was visiting
from Iowa.
Clell was totally
smitten by
Betsy's breathtaking beauty!! Surprising himself,

he was able to overcome his shyness around Betsy. He even did something he had never done before in his life. He envisioned Betsy in a wedding gown walking down the aisle to join him in holy matrimony!

Betsy and Mr. and Mrs. Olson were sitting around on the front porch while Clell played the good host, serving lemonade and cookies. He went into the house to get another pitcher of lemonade on this hot day. When he returned, Betsy was not on the porch. When he asked her whereabouts, Mrs. Olson pointed to the "little house".

"Oh, no!" Clell exclaimed. "Mrs. Olson, please hurry and go tell your niece not to pull the chain!"

Mrs. Olson started down the path, but she was too late! With a wild scream, Betsy came flying out through the door with her clothes in disarray!! It seems that Clell had not had any backhouse visitors in a few weeks. In the meantime, a mama deermouse had chosen this nice clean container of sawdust as a good place to bring up a family. Betsy had been showered with not only sawdust, but a litter of baby mice, who probably didn't like what had happened any better than Betsy did!!

Betsy's first reaction was to leave immediately, but seeing that Clell was so obviously sorry for what had happened, she changed her mind. Later, she could even laugh over the matter. She stayed at her aunt and uncle's for the rest of the summer, and during that time, Clell and Betsy were constant companions. Finally, Clell managed to screw up his courage and asked Betsy to marry him. Much to his surprise, she said yes.

Clell never pulled another prank the rest of his life!!

CHAPTER FIVE

THE DOPEY DUO

atrick and Michael O'Connell, alias "Pat" and "Mike", came to the area south of Minneapolis in 1883. They tried their hand at numberous jobs with little success.

As often happens when men are down on their luck, they turned to a life of crime - mostly petty thievery. They weren't violent men by nature and, in fact, looked down on such goings on. They never held up banks or even used guns. But the two were apt to steal anything that wasn't tied down that they could carry.

Pat and Mike didn't get rich but they did make a living at their newly chosen career. That is until the night they broke into the hardware store at Hastings. Unbeknownst to them, the owner lived upstairs and heard the noise. He was a big, burly man and when the thieves were looking down the barrels of a 12-guage shotgun, they gave up with little more than a murmur. The owner tied them up and went for the sheriff.

The O'Connell brothers were sentenced to five years in the state penitentiary. The prison officials considered them model prisoners, but the truth was, Pat and Mike felt they had it pretty good there. They didn't have to worry where each meal was coming from.

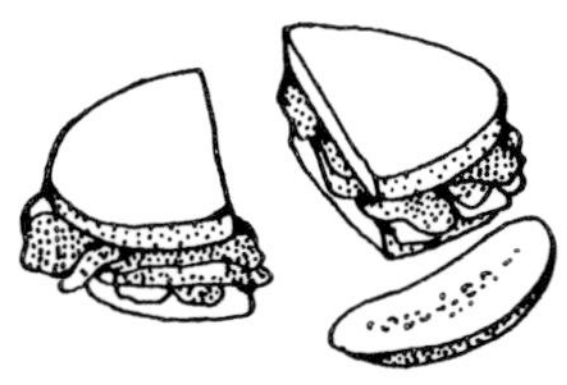

They had a half-way decent place to lay their heads and the brothers didn't even mind the company they kept.

One day in late Spring, the two petty thieves overheard a plan for a prison break. They didn't pay too much attention until the leader decided they had heard too much and would have to go along. The pair tried to decline the invitation but were given an offer they couldn't refuse. Either come along or end up very dead. The leader didn't want anyone to know their plans except those involved.

So, one night the first part of June they made their break. Pat and Mike were two of the lucky ones to escape. Some of the others weren't quite so lucky and fell by the wayside in a hail storm of .44 bullets.

After hiding out in the woods that night, they

wondered what they were supposed to do. The brothers hadn't planned that far ahead, as they were content in prison. Now, being thrown out on their own and hunted men they were a bit scared!

The two escaped convicts made their way to the nearest town. They arrived in the cover of darkness the second night since getting out. The

men broke into a grocery store and stole something to eat. Pat spied a tin box on a shelf and stuffed it into his pocket.

Meanwhile, prison authorities and the sheriff and his posse were on the trail of the O'Connell boys. They figured they were about half a day behind the convicts, when told about the breakin. Dogs were brought in to follow the "desperados" trail.

Pat and Mike were making their way back to the St. Paul/Minneapolis area. This might not have proven to be too smart, since they were known in the area. But the O'Connell brothers had never gotten any awards for having too many brains. They were smart enough to know that dogs were probably picking up their scent by now, though. So, the escapees figured they'd better come up with faster transportation than Shank's ponies.

"Ah don't think Ah kin go 'nother step, Pat," Mike informed his brother. "Let's stop here fer the night. They ain't gonna be huntin' fer us in tha dark!"

"We cain't jest sleep outten tha open, Mike," Pat remarked.

"Let's jist see whet's up ahead under them trees. Ya kin make it thet far, cain'tcha?"

"S'pose so, but not much futher."

So the two convicts walked on. When they reach-ed the area, the brothers found an ideal hiding place - a cemetery!

"Ah don't wanna bunk down with no ghosts!!"
Mike informed Pat.

"Oh, come on, Mike, tain't tha dead ya have ta
worry 'bout. It's tha livin'!"

So the pair of brothers spent a few hours getting
some much needed shuteye under a tree near the
cemetery gate. At the crack of dawn they were
up and getting ready to take off again. But not
before Pat dug out the tin container from his
pocket. Opening it, he started walking backwards,
sprinkling the contents onto the ground. Then they
broke brush getting out of there.

The sheriff and posse were also out at the crack
of dawn with the dogs in hot pursuit. Within a few
short hours, they arrived at the cemetery. The dogs
scented the escapees until they got near the gate.
Then the dogs began to yelp, run around and, in
general, to act rather weird!

One of the possee member, who was superstitious,
rolled his eyes heavenward and muttered, "Oh,
Lawd, have mercy! Those dogs done found a
ghost!"

"What are ya talkin' 'bout, Mose Jasper?" the sheriff
asked.

"We ain't s'posed ta be here! It's sacred ground. Thet's why them dogs are actin' up!"

But the sheriff found the empty tin container Pat had thrown away near the gate and picked it up.

"Here's what's causin' them dogs to act up," the lawman said. "Red pepper! They covered up their trail with it. Now, those dogs ain't gonna be worth a continental hooey with that stuff up their noses. Might just as well quit for now!"

The sheriff and posse packed it in for the time be-ing. Meanwhile, Pat and Mike were several miles away. They were foot-weary and hungry.

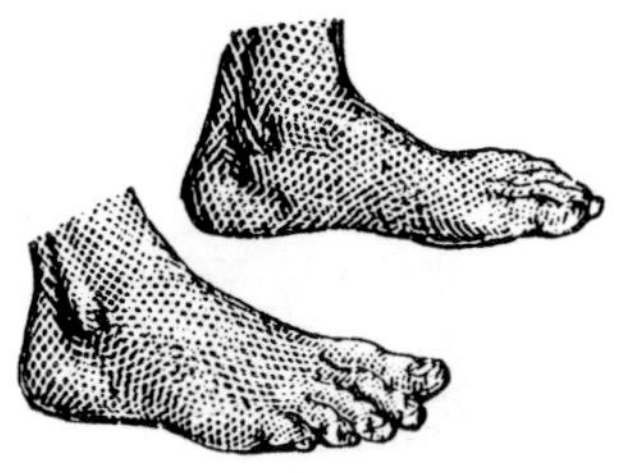

"We've gotta git us a horse and wagon some-wheres," Mike told Pat. "Ah jist can't go on like this. Ah think Ah got a hitch in mah gitty-up!!"

"Me, too, Mike! Me, too. Let's sit down an' rest a spell. Ah think uh must have a dozen blisters on my feet!!"

The pair of convicts sat down on an old log.

"Whew! Ah don't know 'bouts you, but Ah shore wish Ah wuz back in prison! Ah'm suh hungry Ah could eat a horse," Pat remarked.

"Here, too. At least we had three squares uh day. Ah swear, mah stumick thinks mah throat's bin cut!!"

Pat frowned and cocked his head to one side. "Listen!! Ah thinks Ah hears chickens. Must be purty close ta a farm. Maybe we kin git us sumthin' ta eat!"

Luckily for the convicts, the owner of the farm was a widow-lady that didn't appear to have both oars in the water. Her eyes were dull and she was slovenly dressed. But at that point, Pat and Mike could have cared less. She was out feeding her chickens when they got there.

She believed their story that they were part of the posse and had been separated from the others when their horses threw them. She fixed them a meal of flapjacks and side pork, with plenty of strong, black coffee. When they were finished, the brothers couldn't remember when they had enjoyed a meal more. They offered to pay her, knowing that they had no money, and hoped she'd refuse. She did, much to their gratitude.

The O'Connell brothers left and made their way
to a neighboring farm. They were desperate to find
horses as their feet were blistered and raw. No one
was at home, so they saddled two horses and took
off down the road. When the convicts were about
a half mile from the farm, they saw a man walking toward them. The brothers stopped to ask
directions.

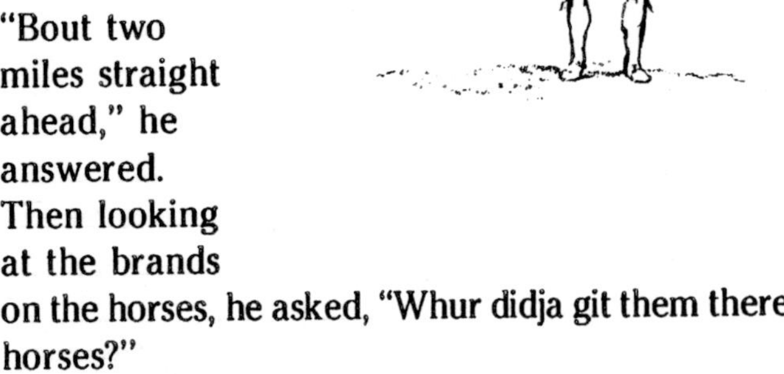

"How far to
the next
town?" Pat
asked the
man.

"Bout two
miles straight
ahead," he
answered.
Then looking
at the brands
on the horses, he asked, "Whur didja git them there
horses?"

"Bought 'em from a man a few miles back," Mike
answered.

"Ah don't b'lieve ya," the man replied. "Them's
mah horses!! Now, jist git yur butts offen 'em!" he
ordered, as he drew his gun.

The convicts did as he said without giving him any
trouble. They just started walking on down the
road, never turning around.

After they had rounded a bend in the road, Pat
spotted a fallen log in a ditch.

"Ah jist have ta rest. My feet hurt suh bad. Ah jist
don't know hows Ah kin walk much futher!!" Mike
said.

The brothers sat down and rested for a while. Then
Pat turned to Mike, pointing his finger up the road.

"Duz mah eyes deceive me or duz Ah see whut
Ah thinks Ah sees?" he asked.

"If ya think ya see a wagon and horses, Ah thinks
yer right!!" Mike replied.

The O'Connell boys got up and started hobbling
toward the horses and wagon. They couldn't see
anyone around, so they climbed aboard, turned
the horses around in the opposite direction and
took off on the run.

Pat and Mike finally decided that horses AND
wagon was not their best means of gettin' around
since they had to stick to the roads. With just
horses, riding through the woods would pose no
problem.

(51)

They unhitched the wagon, and rode the horses bareback.

By this time, the brothers were near Cambridge in the extreme eastern side of Minnesota. They had changed their minds about going to St. Paul and decided instead to cross into Wisconsin. Along the way, they broke into several grocery stores in order to quiet their stomach rumblings.

Heading due east from Cambridge, they arrived in Cumberland, Wisconsin in a couple of days. Cumberland was known as a very "rough and ready" town during this time. The escaped convicts saw many tough looking rowdies roaming around, dressed in all kinds of garb as if for a costume contest. So, the two convicts calmly walked around town looking at the preparations for various celebrations, as it was the 4th of July!

It finally occurred to them that they were still dressed in their prison outfits!! They might blend in, as
their beards had grown considerably in the past
month, but they were afraid of being recognized.
They hurried in behind a saloon, quickly shucked
out of their convict clothing, and threw them into
a crate in the alley.

Pat and Mike O'Connell, the "desperadoes", emerged out onto the streets of Cumberland dressed in
only their birthday suits and a smile!

Students of the history of Cumberland would be
interested to know that these boys in their new
chilly costumes attracted less attention then they
had when they had their prison "costumes" on. All
of which certainly reveals to us today something
about Cumberland of the late 1800's!

CHAPTER SIX

"MA" TURNER

omewhere in the vicinity of Plateville, in southwestern Wisconsin, near the turn of the century, lived Pansy Turner. Woe be unto anyone that ever called her Pansy. In her late years, she grew to hate that sissy name.

"Ma" Turner was a big woman, standing five-foot-nine in her bare feet. She had some two hundred fifty pounds of muscle covering her large frame. "Ma" was one of those gutsy females that helped settle this country.

Local legend had it that "Ma" went bear-huntin' with a switch! Or just "grinned them down" — like Daniel Boone. But the truth was, she was better with a gun then most men. And she could shoot from the hip, if push came to shove. Her first husband, Thom Olson, had taught her that.

"Ma" was born in eastern Ohio. Thom Olson had come through there on business and completely fooled 17-year old Pansy Stevens. She thought he had a lot of money. Not until they were married and he carried her off to his "mansion" in the wilds of Wisconsin did she discover the truth. His "mansion" was a three-room tumbled down shack. His "estate" consisted of a few acres of rocky land on a lake close to town.

Pansy Stevens Olson was outraged. Even at the young age of 17-years, she had a temper that could make a big man quiver. Thom Olson was indeed lucky to escape with his life for lying to Pansy. If she had had the where-with-all to get back east, she would have gone. But she didn't and her lying husband wouldn't have given it to her, so she was stuck. Besides, she was expecting their one and only child. The baby had been conceived on the way to Wisconsin. Once in their "mansion", Pansy informed Thom that if he ever dared to touch her again, he was dead!

So, the two lived like brother and sister. They grubbed out a meager living. Pansy dug up a garden area, piling up the rocks which she later

turned into a rock garden. She was able to raise
a half-way decent garden and a neighbor lady
showed her how to can.

Pansy's baby was weakly from his birth on
Thanksgiving Day - which she blamed on Thom.
She told him that even his seed was no good. The
baby, which was named Ethan Joseph after Pansy's
father, died before Christmas. Although she was
grief-stricken, she wasn't surprised.

Pansy made the best of her marriage - after a
fashion. She tried to learn everything that would
be of use. She also talked Thom into buying a cow,
a horse, and some chickens.

Thom taught Pansy to shoot a gun. She ended up being a better shot than her husband. And when she got "cabin-fever", she went hunting. This tough lady put away a considerable amount of dried or canned game for the next winter.

Thom built a boat which wasn't too seaworthy. One day that summer, Thom went out on the lake and never returned. The boat was found close to shore, but Thom's body was never found. Everyone just assumed that he had drowned. Pansy wasn't sure at the time, but didn't really care one way or the other.

Being the woman that she was, Pansy never asked for help. Things went along pretty much the same as before. The only thing missing was Thom.

She had been a widow nigh onto ten years when William Turner appeared in her life. Pansy took an instant dislike to him, or so she tried to tell herself. She felt he was too smug - and too handsome. She had driven her horse and wagon into town on one of her rare visits. Pansy needed some

material for a couple of new dresses as hers were getting pretty threadbare.

Pansy tied "Old Patch" up to the hitching post in front of the general store. She was thinking about what color material she'd look at, when a gentleman approached her.

"Say, ma'am, could you direct me to the nearest hotel?" a smooth masculine voice asked.

"Ya speakin' ta me?" Pansy inquired.

"Yes, ma'm. I asked directions to the nearest hotel."

"Yah, Ah heard ya," she replied. "Ah thinks it's a couple of blocks down thet way," Pansy said, pointing a finger to the east. "Only one in town, but Ah don't git in town too often and hain't had no reason ta stay at a hotel, so Ah ain't sure."

"Do they have a dining room there?" the man asked.

"Don't rightfully know. Ya'll jist halfta ask 'em, won'tcha?"

Pansy started toward the door of the store.

"Pardon me, ma'am, but would you give me the honor of dining with me?" he asked.

"Ah done et. Besides, Ah don't know ya, Mister!!" she replied haughtily, and walked into the store, slamming the door behind her.

The man stood and stared after her with one eyebrow raised and a puzzled look on his face. He then shook his head, as if clearing away the cobwebs — and then started to walk in the direction of the hotel.

Meanwhile, Pansy Olson was looking at the bolts of material but her mind wasn't on the fabric. She

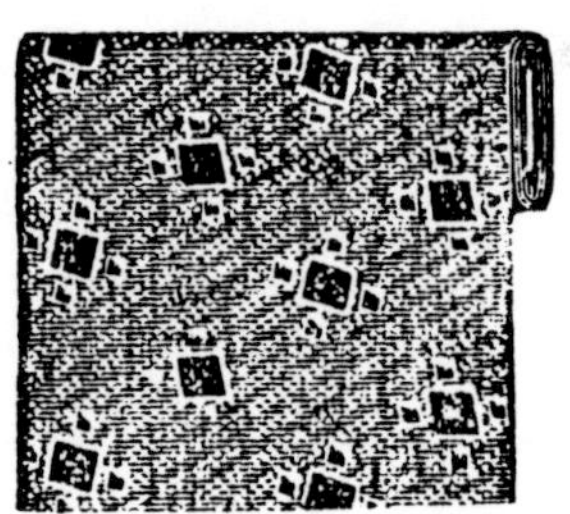

kept running the conversation over and over in her mind. Maybe she shouldn't have been quite so snippy! She didn't want to admit to herself that she'd been attracted to the man. And besides, what business did he have inviting her - a perfect stranger - to eat with him?

"Kin I help ya, Miz Olson?" the store owner said interrupting Pansy's thoughts.

"Oh! Yah. Ah'd like four yards of each of these two materials," Pansy answered, not paying much attention to which ones she'd picked out.

Pansy paid for her purchase and left. When she got outside by the wagon, she looked up the street toward the hotel. But she couldn't see the gentleman she was looking for.

"What'd ya expect, Pansy Olson? After the way ya treated him, didja think he'd be out here waitin' fer ya?" she asked herself. "Jist git yourself fer home like yur s'posed ta, and quit your moonin'!"

Pansy couldn't get her encounter with the gentlemen out of her mind. And like many people who live alone, she carried on a conversation with herself.

"Yer jist bein' foolish, Pansy Olson!! Why, ya don't even know his name, let alone anything else 'bout him. Are ya gettin' so tetched in the head by livin' out here alone that ya start actin' like a damned fool when some man jist happens to speak to ya?"

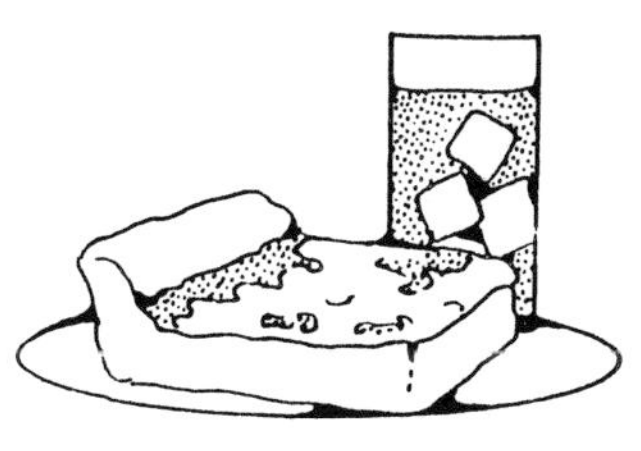

"Yah, but he did more than jist speak. He asked me ta have sumthin' ta eat with him, 'member?"

"Yah, but he wuz jist bein' polite 'cause ya give him directions, thet's all!"

"Maybe yes, maybe no."

"Now see here, Pansy Olson!! Ya ain't no ravin' beauty thet a fine gentleman like thet's gonna throw himself at yer feet! Smarten up!"

The next day, Pansy realized that she didn't have thread to match her new material.

"Well, as much as Ah hates ta go, guess Ah'll jist halfta git some thread," she told herself.

Pansy put on her least faded dress, brushed her hair and powdered her nose - something she hadn't done in years. She decided she looked a little better than she had yesterday.

"Miz Olson," the store owner greeted her as she walked in. "How nice ta see ya agin so soon. How kin Ah help ya?"

"Fergot to git thread. And, maybe Ah'll jist browse a little. Might find sumthin' else."

"Jist help yurself, Miz Olson. Take all the time ya need."

Pansy dawdled around, looking at all the "purties", such as ribbon-bedecked hats, and ornate pen-

dants. When she reached the bolts of material, she looked at some frilly, light blue, feminine fabric which she had not noticed before.

"Say, ma'm, that's awfully pretty material. Just matches your eyes," said a familiar voice behind Pansy.

She noticeably jumped and a dark pink spread over her neck and cheeks.

"Oh, I'm sorry, ma'm. I didn't mean to surprise you that much. Please forgive me!"

Pansy stammered and stuttered and felt like she was making a complete blithering idiot of herself. She had wanted to make a better impression on him than she had yesterday, but she sure wasn't doing it this way, she told herself. She finally found her voice.

"Why - why - thank ya, sir. Ah-Ah didn't see ya come up!"

"I must introduce myself. My name is Turner. Bill Turner. And what is yours, my dear?"

"Pansy Olson," she answered.

"Well, Miss Olson. Or is it Mrs.?"

"It's really Mrs., Ah guess."

"Mrs., you guess? I'm afraid I don't understand."

"Ah'm a widder, Mr. Turner."

"Oh, I'm so sorry, Mrs. Olson."

There was an embarrased lag in the conversation while Penny fingered the light blue material. Finally, she pulled herself to her full height and turned to Bill Turner.

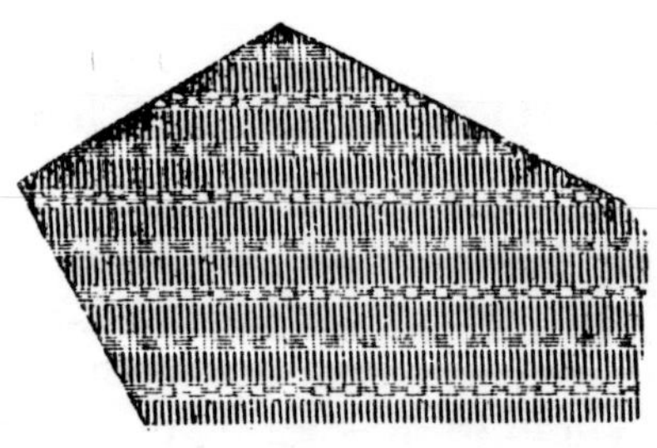

"Well, sir. Ah guess Ah'd better git mah thread and needles and git fer home. Gotta git them dresses made purty soon."

"Aren't you going to get this material, Miss Pansy? You would really look so lovely in it."

"Naw, Ah don't go no place ta wear it. Besides, it's too fancy fer me. Ah can't afford nuthin' thet purty."

"I see. Well, now. You turned me down for dinner yesterday. Is there a chance you might do me the honor today?"

"It would be mah pleasure, Mr. Turner," Pansy said. "Jest let me git mah stuff and Ah'll be right with ya."

"Please call me Bill, fair lady."

So Bill and Pansy had a delightful meal, each filling in the details of themselves to the other. He was a business man - so he told Pansy. What he neglected to tell her was that his business took him to many different towns, usually just ahead of the sheriff. Bill Turner was a card shark!

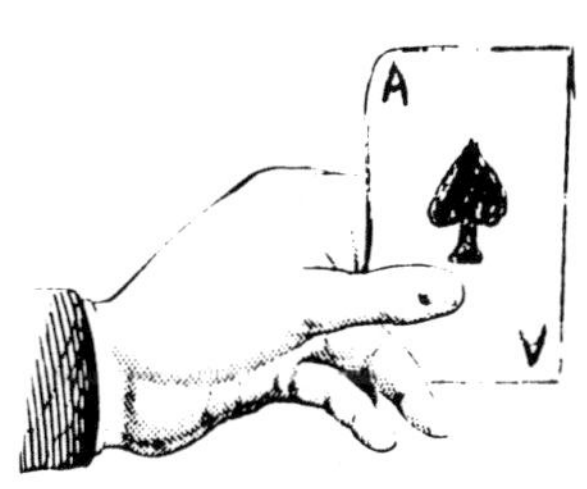

Over the next few days, Bill and Pansy saw quite a lot of each other. Then one day he brought her a package. When she opened it, her eyes filled with tears. It was the light blue material - enough to make her a fancy dress!

"Ah don't know how ta thank ya, but where would Ah wear it?"

"How about to a wedding? Our wedding. I'm asking you to marry me, Pansy Olson."

Through her tears, Pansy somehow blubbered a "yes", hugging the material to her.

Two weeks later, Bill and Pansy tied the knot — much to everyone's surprise. Most of the townspeople know of Bill Turner's profession, especially the men. They'd lost enough to him in card games! They wondered how Pansy cold possibly have gotten herself involved with him. But the truth was, since Pansy did not indulge in gossip, she wasn't aware that Bill was a gambler. And at that point — it might not have made any difference.

Everything went well for the newly-weds for a week or so. Then Bill started getting itchy fingers to be back at work. He told Pansy that he had clients to see in the evenings. She was gullible enough to believe him.

One night about a month after their wedding, Bill Turner didn't come home. Pansy waited until daylight and then hitched up "Old Patch". Arriving at the sheriff's office, she was told the bad news. Bill Turner had been shot during a poker game. He had been caught cheating!

The grief-stricken Pansy, although thoroughly confused, laid Bill to rest in the cemetery on the hill, alongside her son. She couldn't believe that she had been taken in again by a man! Her grief eventually turned to bitterness, then to hate!

Bound and determined to never again get taken in by a man's sweet talk, Pansy shut all men from her life as best she could. She would not allow anyone to call her Pansy anymore, either. Said that's what got her into trouble before, 'cause it was such a sissy name. So, she became known as "Ma" Turner.

She seldom went into town and if she did, rarely talked to anyone, especially men, and then, strictly on business.

One day, some five years after Bill's death, she was in town at the bank. As "Ma" was coming out to her wagon, Ephraim Dunn, the town drunk, thought he'd see if maybe she'd softened up a bit. Stumbling over to her, he put a hand on "Ma's" arm. With one swat, he ended up flat on the ground, with "Ma" glaring at him.

"Jeez, Ma, Ah jest wanted a little kiss!" Ephraim said.

"Ma's" reply set him, and all the other men standing around watching, straight on the subject ever after. "Kiss? Why ya dirty old drunk!! Ah'll tell you and all men right here and now — AH WOULDN'T GIVE YA THE SWEAT OFFEN "OLD PATCH'S" SOUTH END!"

CHAPTER SEVEN

GRANDPA HARRY'S SPECTACLES

ack during the early 1900's, especially in the rural areas of Northern Wisconsin, folks didn't get to town too often. They relied on canvassing salesman with their black suitcases to bring the "needful things".

Grandpa Harry was getting on in years and for quite some time had been having a hard time reading the newspaper. He kept saying he was going to have to get some reading glasses, but kept putting it off, as some folks do.

Grandpa Harry was also known to take a nip from the jug on occasion, in fact, several. One day in early May, he was sitting out on the front porch in his favorite rocker. He had taken a couple of nips of homemade blackberry wine for his "rumatiz" he said. A salesman pulled up in front of the house in his horsedrawn carriage. He hurried down the path and up to the porch where Grandpa

Harry was just sitting and rocking, and occasionally taking a nip for medicinal purposes. The salesman laid his suitcase down on the floor of the porch and opened it up.

Grandpa had a hard time seeing all the "goodies" the salesman had to offer, partly due to his failing eyesight and partly due to the blackberry wine. He saw some things that sparkled, but what really

caught his eye were several pairs of reading glasses. Grandpa Harry tried all of them on and then finally chose a pair that fit his needs. He didn't have much money on him, but Grandma Bessie dug out some hoarded change from a jar in the cupboard. So, Grandpa Harry finally had his much-needed reading glasses!

A few weeks later, while reading the local weekly, he read a headline which seemed to fairly jump out at him: "JEWEL THIEF FROM BELOIT CANVASSING AREA COUNTIES"!!

The article went on to describe the thief. It also stated that the sheriff was close on his trail and what the penalty would be for anyone found having bought any of the stolen goods!

Grandpa was pretty upset and had quite a few nips out of his jug. But he decided he wasn't about to turn himself in. NO SIREE!! He needed those glasses and he didn't want to part with them - NO WAY!! Anyhow, if the sheriff was on the thief's trail, he didn't need no help from him!

But apparently the sheriff wasn't as close as he had thought. Several months went by without anything further mentioned. Everyone in the area forgot about the jewel thief, except for Grandpa Harry.

Well, you know how coincidences happen sometimes. The local church got a new minister. Reverend Andrews made some calls to get acquainted with the members of his congregation.

Grandpa was sitting out on the porch in his favorite rocker although it was rather cool. His glasses were on the table in the front room next to the newspaper. When Reverend Andrews started up the path, all Grandpa Harry noticed was the parson's black bag! He liked to come unglued! Struggling up from his rocker, he met the new minister at the edge of the porch.

"Well, now, young feller! Ya got a whole lotta nerve! Just how fur is the sheriff behind ya?"

Not waiting for an answer, the old man reached around the doorway in the house and produced a shot gun. Grandpa Harry couldn't shoot too well, what with his eye sight and all, but he could shoot straight enough to burn the preacher's south end.

This was the first and last visit from the new minister!

CHAPTER EIGHT

FREDDIE THE FROG

ill Peterson had always been a high-spirited youngster. He lived with his parents and older sister, Kate, at the edge of one of the little lakes that dot Crow Wing County in central Minnesota.

Bill was one of those kind of boys that delight in putting the end of girls' braids in the inkwell. Or put garter snakes in the teacher's desk drawer. He was constantly in trouble, both at school and at home.

This "Prince of Pranks" was a Huckleberry Finn type kid, and therefore, enjoyed spending a lot of his time down by the lake, catching frogs. One late afternoon, he caught the grand-daddy of all frogs. He

wasn't sure at first what he was going to do with it. Then he spied his sister, Kate, bending over the washboard in the laundry tub, out in the yard near the well. The tub was setting on a four-legged stool which had seen better days. Kate's back was toward Bill as he crept up behind her.

Before Kate even knew that Bill was around, that big old frog was down the back of her dress and Bill was out of arm's length. Kate screamed, lost her balance, and fell forward over the washboard into the tub. That was more weight than that weak-legged stool could hold. Kate, the washtub, and the wet clothes all went spilling onto the yard! Kate was screaming her lungs out when Ma Peterson came running out of the house. Bill was holding his stomach, fairly splitting his seams from laughing. Ma Peterson took one look and knew that Bill had done it again! Grabbing him by the ear, she roughly escorted him to the back door.

"Git yer behind in there and Ah'll tend ta ya later!" Ma Peterson yelled at Bill.

She then rushed over to Kate, who was floundering in the washtub trying to get rid of the frog. Ma Peterson reached down the back of Kate's dress and retrieved the squirming green critter and set it loose.

After getting the mess cleaned up and consoling Kate, Ma went into the house to settle up with her wayward son.

"William Peterson, yer gonna be tha death of me yet!! Cain't ya be good jist once in a while? Lawdy me, Ah jist don't know who ya takes after! Shore ain't nobody on mah side uv the family! This time, ya went too far. When yer Pa gits back from Shephard, Ah'm gonna let him deal with ya!"

Bill was a little shook up over his mother's decision. She never dealt out too harsh a punishment, but his Pa was another matter. He could remember the few lickings he'd gotten from Pa Peterson and his rear-end still smarted just thinking about them. He thought about running away from home.

"Meanwhile, young man — ya jist sit right thar on
thet chair and don'tcha move till yer Pa gits home,"
his mother warned him.

Well, there went his idea of running away, right
out the window!!

After Pa Peterson unhitched his team from the
wagon, he came into the house, bringing in the
groceries he'd gotten in Shephard.

Pa looked at Bill sitting so quietly on the chair and
figured he was in trouble again. After his wife told
him what Bill had done, he KNEW his son was in
trouble! Taking off his belt, he invited Bill out to
the woodshed.

"Bill, this here is gonna hurt me worsen you. But,
son, Ah gotta do sumthin' ta make ya remember
the next time ya git mischief-makin' in yer head."

Ma Peterson could hear Bill's yells in the house.
She covered her ears and shook her head. She felt

guilty, but also knew that something had to be done about Bill's pranks.

Bill was put to bed without any supper. But the licking made a big impression on his mind as well as his backside.

After that episode with the belt Bill calmed himself down and even attended school on a regular basis.

He still liked to spend time down by the lake. One day in early summer, Bill caught a big old frog. Not as big as the one he put down Kate's dress, though. He attached one end of a string to the frog's leg and the other to a stick he had stuck in the ground. Bill would catch flies and bugs for the frog, which he named Freddie.

During the long summer days, Bill spent his time down by the lake, teaching Freddie lots of tricks. By the end of summer, Bill thought it was time to show his family Freddie's antics.

Bill wasn't quite sure just how he was going to smuggle Freddie into the house. Maybe he could carry him in underneath his shirttail. But no one was around when he got to the house. 'They've probably gone into town,' he thought. So, Bill decided to just wait until they got back. It was quite some time though, so he started to put Freddie through his paces.

Bill was thinking so much about how smart he was to have been able to teach his frog all these tricks that he didn't hear his father's footsteps on the porch. Freddie was just making his leap over the willow branch that Bill was holding when Pa Peterson opened the door.

Freddie completed his leap, landing at the toe of Pa Peterson's right foot!

"Carnsarned kid and his frogs!!" Mr. Peterson exclaimed, as he brought his #12 boot down into a

stomp — sending the talented Freddie to frog
heaven!!!

CHAPTER NINE

THE GOLDEN APPLES

ed River serves, among other things, as the boundary between North Dakota and western Minnesota. Some, fifty years ago, a "strange" bunch of rocks were found along the banks of the Red River near Robbin.

Bert Anderson, "Punky" Willard, and Tom Godfrey were enjoying a good June day. No school, no chores, just play. They had a nice, big can of worms to go fishing with, but the fish weren't biting so well. So, they stuck the ends of their willow

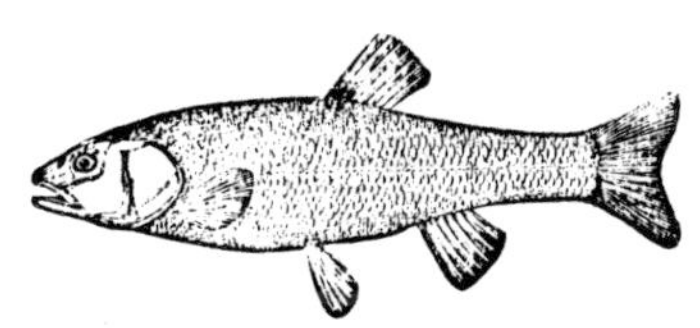

poles in the mud along the riverbank and went "frog chasin' ". This was a whole lot of fun for three nine-year-old boys.

"Hey, look at that big old frog! Betcha can't catch it!" Bert yelled at the other two boys.

"Betcha a nickel I kin," Punky yelled back.

The three boys ran off after that big, old green hoppy critter as fast as they could, slipping and sliding on the muddy river bank. Bert didn't believe that Punky could catch that frog, so he wasn't much afraid of losing his nickel. Punky was a little on the fat-side and couldn't run very fast. Bert didn't think his friend could even catch a cold unless he worked hard at it.

Punky, graceful child that he was, managed to stub

his toe on a tree root and fell "kersplat" right on his belly. It hurt, but Punky was determined not to cry in front of his pals. While he was lying there, trying to regain his dignity, his eyes fastened on a rock about the size of an apple just a bare few inches from his nose.

"Boy," he thought to himself, "am I glad I didn't hit that! Woulda splattered my nose all over my face!"

Staring at the rock intently, Punky noticed that it was shiny in spots. Forgetting about his clumsiness, he got up as quickly as possible. Picking up the rock, which was quite heavy, he turned it around and around in his hands.

"Hey, guys!" Punky yelled at the other two. "Looka what I got!"

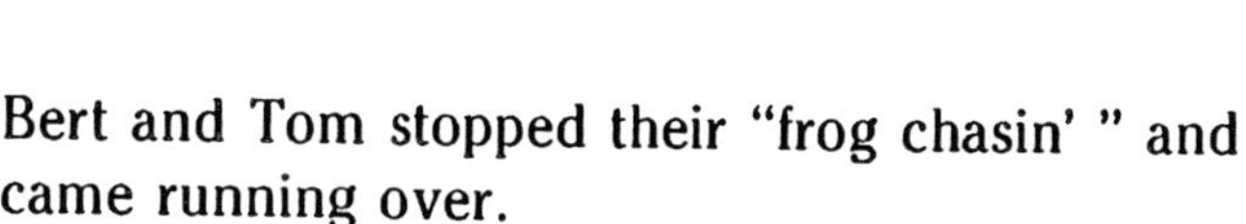

Bert and Tom stopped their "frog chasin' " and came running over.

"Just an old rock," Tom said.

"No 'taint," Punky informed him, turning the rock over in his hands. "See how it shines in spots."

Punky found a stick and started scraping the dirt
and mud from his rock. The more he scraped, the
more shiny spots appeared.

"Hey, 'Punk-old-buddy', I think yer right. Sure is
purty," Bert remarked.

The boys looked around and saw several other
"shiny" rocks in the area. They cleaned them off
as best they could and stuffed them in their
pockets. When the boys had as many as they could
carry, they started off - droopy-drawered - for
home, their fishing poles forgotten.

The frog-chasin' trio was quite a ways from home
and it seemed a whole lot further, what with the
weight of all those rocks.

Punky was a sight to behold when he got home.
The river mud all over his front side, feet and
hands caused his mother to let out an exasperated
yell when she saw him.

"Punky Willard! Just look at you! Where in the
world have you bin?"

He showed her the shiny rock together with the others he dug out of his pants pockets.

"Where did you git these rocks, son?" she asked.

"Down by the river," the boy replied.

Mrs. Willard examined the rocks excitedly. She then rushed to the phone, calling first Mrs. Anderson and then Mrs. Godfrey, inviting them and the boys over to her house.

There was mass confusion, what with everyone trying to talk at once. Finally, Mrs. Willard held up her hands to silence the group.

"First off, we need to know where these "rocks" came from. Second, we need to know if you kids kin find the place agin."

"I think I kin find it," Tom ventured. "We left our fishin' poles stuck in the mud purty close ta where we found these shiny rocks."

"Well, I think we'd better wait until the menfolk git home. By then, it'd probably be too late to go lookin'. But since tomorrow's Saturday, maybe we kin all go then! What say?"

Everyone agreed. They'd wait till the next day to

go rock hunting. In the meantime, they'd just stick to making plans.

But, as often happens, Mother Nature didn't cooperate with these plans. Along about evening, the sky blackened and the rain came down in buckets. Mr. Willard got wet coming home. It rained all night and the better part of the next day. But Sunday dawned full of sunshine and warm air. It was really muddy, but after church, and changing their clothes, the three families met to go hunting.

After picking their way down to where the boys thought they had been fishing, everyone looked around.

There was no sign of the willow poles anywhere! Apparently, the river had washed them downstream, along with the can of worms. All the rocks along the riverbank were covered with a thick layer of mud. There wasn't a shiny rock to be seen!

After searching around for quite awhile, the group finally gave up. Either they weren't looking in the right spot or the boys had found all the shiny rocks there had been, the adults decided. But the boys kept insisting there were "thousands" of those rocks shining in the sunlight. The parents agreed there wasn't any thing to back this up, so they all returned home.

After having the "rocks" tested, the parents suspicions were confirmed. They were gold nuggets! And they brought enough to help all three families out for a long time.

Folks figured that the nuggets might have washed ashore from a sunken boat. Or maybe they were buried by persons unknown. Whatever became of the rest of these shiny rocks - if, indeed, there were more - is not known. What is known is that gold had never before or since been found around there.

CHAPTER TEN

THE WATERY GRAVE

The quiet waters of Lake Superior were disturbed by as a large pleasure craft moving swiftly in the night heading for Rossport, Ontario. The owner, a magnate from Ohio, planned to lay over for the night there before going on to Port Arthur and Fort William. But little did the skipper know that the darkness of night hid a treacherous shoal a few feet under the water!

The craft weighed 384 tons and was 250 feet long. It pushed hard on the rock ledge, driving her bow high in the air. Although undamaged, she couldn't back off.

Upset over this turn of events, the owner was forced to abandon his yacht temporarily. He made his way to Rossport in a powered lifeboat. Once on land, he contacted the Great Lakes Dredging and Salvage Company, who in turn, sent out their powerful steam-tug to free the stranded craft.

Upon their arrival, the owner insisted that all he wanted them to do was to pull the yacht off the shoal and not wait for a diver to inspect the boat.

The tug captain obeyed the millionaire's wishes. He hitched a line to the pleasure craft and steadily took up the strain. The vessel finally slid slowly off the ledge. The owner felt that Lady Luck was with him, but quickly changed his mind when the boat did not stop. It filled with water and then sank to the bottom of Lake Superior, some 300 feet below!

Several attempts were made to salvage the yacht, but she was far beyond their reach. They dream-ed of her cargo, which was rumored to include precious jewels, silverware, and a large supply of rare liquors.

So far, their dreams of wealth have turned to only wisps of hope.

CHAPTER ELEVEN

CAGEY CHAFLIN

ish Creek is a town in Northern Wisconsin. It sits amid bluffs on both the east and west sides. The first settler here, Increase Chaflin, was a fringe-whiskered, rock-jawed gentleman from New York. He built a large, two-story log cabin overlooking the harbor in 1844.

Chaflin had lived at Little Sturgeon Bay before coming to Fish Creek. There, he bred horses and traded with the Indians. At first, he had a good relationship with the Indians. Then his hired man, Robert Stevenson, married his eldest daughter, and took over the trading. Stevenson treated the natives badly, plying them with liquor and then cheating them unmercifully!

Finally, the Indians had had enough of this treatment. A group under Silver Band found and overpowered Chaflin.

Knowing that he was in a position to be parted from his scalp, Chaflin said, "Now, Silver Band you and I have always gotten along real good, hain't we? I want ta continue being friends with you and your tribe. What say we talk 'bout things over a keg of whiskey?"

Chief Silver Band agreed that this would help negotiations quite a bit. 

Chaflin went into the trading post and rolled out a keg. Much to the Indians' surprise, when Chaflin ripped off the cover, the keg was full of gunpowder!

Standing with one foot on the keg and a lighted torch in his hand, Chaflin yelled at the startled Indians.

"Okay, now ya dadburned critters! If ya want ta

try some double-dealin' on me—why, I'll blow ya
all ta Kingdom Come! So ya better listen closely
ta what I've got ta say 'bout how we can come ta
some kind of peace agreement. If ya don't wanna
go along with it, then I'll just touch this here torch
to the gunpowder and blooey! fried Indian!!"

Needless to say, the frightened Indians agreed with
EVERYTHING Chaflin said!

CHAPTER TWELVE

OSHKOSH LUMBERJACKS, BY GOSH

shkosh lies in a marshy area where the Upper Fox River flows into Lake Winnebago. It was besieged by fires in 1858, 1866, and 1874. It was rebuilt with wood each time, but after the fire of 1875, the damage was so great that it was rebuilt with stone and brick.

Industry was only briefly interrupted by these catastrophes. Logging went on unabated. But the timberline kept receding. Then it became necessary to build dams on the Wolf River in order to save the water for spring drives. Mill owners could begin operations only after the logs had been delivered to the millponds. Towards the end of the 1870's, manufacturing and milling from rough timber became more worthwhile than transporting logs. Lumbermen were becoming rich. Oshkosh was known as the leading sash and door center of the world, and was nicknamed "Sawdust City".

In those days, payday saw the lumberjacks come roaring into the city. Their first stop was at Otto Naus' saloon at the foot of Main Street. In order to keep his floor from being ripped to pieces by

the lumberjacks' cleated boots, Old Otto had three inches of sawdust spread on the floor. The lumberjacks would work their way up Main Street, hitting the saloons.

Ole Knudstrum, one of the burly, big-mouthed lumberjacks, was accompanied by his latest love, Sonja Anderson, one night. They, and several other couples were hitting all the saloons. They got tired of the noisy brawls in each place they went, so they decided to make a little fun of their own.

The men hired buckboards and bought a keg of whiskey. The lumberjacks loaded it into the back of one of the buckboards and then picked up their lady-loves. They all went whooping and hollering down to the Upper Fox River.

The women had brought along some blankets, which they spread underneath the trees. Next, the keg of whiskey was plugged. There was a lot of yelling and singing. Some of the outlying towns-people were annoyed by the ruckus.

Someone in the group suggested going for a swim. There was a lot of cheering and clothes went fly-ing everywhere. The water was a little cold but it did nothing to sober them up or cool their passion.

The party broke up in the wee hours of the morn-ing. A number of hurry-up weddings resulted from this little escapade.

But as the timberline receded, so did this type of goings-on. And the brawls also moved northward, to the delight of the townswomen of Oshkosh— by gosh!!

CHAPTER THIRTEEN

ALLEN BRADLEY —
THE GENIAL GIANT

ills Rock—in Door County, Wisconsin—is at the tip of the peninsula which overlooks Lake Michigan. Many Nordic and Icelandic people left the barren shores of their home to settle there. It is a fishing village and the home of Scandinavians who, for generations, have fished the lake for a living. Along the waterfront small boats are moored, with

nets drying on the rocks. Off to the side are the weathered sheds where fish are cleaned and nets

are strung. Every day, the men still put out in their
small boats loaded to the gill and set out nets miles
from shore. At night, they bring home their catch
for either shipment or sale to the tourists who visit
the sheds and make their choice of perch, trout,
or whitefish.

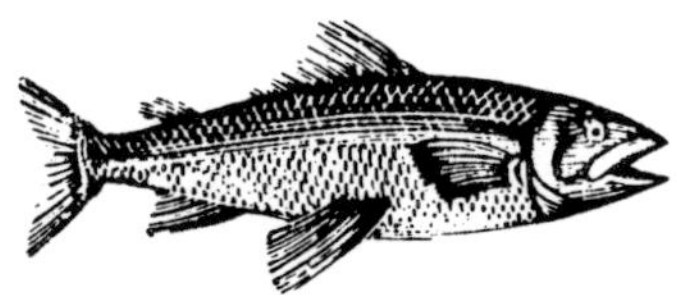

In the 1830's, an Irishman named Allen Bradley
came to Gills Rock. Bradley was a giant of a man,
standing six-foot-six. His chest measured more than
four feet around and his hands were as broad as
shovels. He wore moccasins because he could find
no shoes to fit him. The settlers referred to him
as "Old Bradley, the timber chap who lives like
an Indian and can cut seven cords of wood in a
day."

He was capable of feats of strength fitting to his
size. Bradley could drag a heavy fishing boat up
on the shore single-handed. He also lifted heavy
rocks and logs. Sometimes he let men cling to his

long, thick beard as he carried them about the room. Once, on a bet, he carried a 250-pound man until the man became weary and let go.

Just for fun, his friends thought up outlandish bets to test his strength. One day, a storekeeper offered Bradley a 496-pound barrel of flour if he could carry it on his back to his home - three miles away. Incredible Bradley not only did so, but stopped to chat with a friend along the way!

CHAPTER FOURTEEN

WALLY FERGUSON'S APE-MEN

n the northeastern corner of Minnesota, perched on the Canadian border, is a secluded area known as the Wilderness Lakes country. In the late 1800's, there were very few cabins to be seen, as most people settled where they could do some farming. Hunting, fishing and trapping was about all that could be done in that wild land.

Most of the settlements arose along the shores of Lake Superior. Back then, a small town named Croftville consisting of a store, a saloon, and a few houses was built near Devil's Track Lake. A dozen cabins were strewn within a twenty-mile area of this town.

Wally Ferguson had worked in a sawmill near Minneapolis in his younger years. Deciding to leave the hustle and bustle of the city behind, Wally headed northeast and built a cabin a few miles from Devil's Track Lake. He loved the seclusion and didn't even mind the harsh winters when he was snowbound. If the snow wasn't too deep, though, he'd put on his snowshoes and a heavy sheepskin coat, and trudge into town to the saloon. Wally had a bit of a problem - he liked to drink. In fact, he was seen more often with a "snootfull" then he was sober.

But for the most part, old Wally was harmless. He seldom got rowdy and folks just considered him a happy drunk.

That's why most people remembered for a long time the day that Wally Ferguson came busting into the saloon, wild-eyed and bushy-haired! He kept yelling over and over something about "them damned ape-men"!

There was several inches of snow on the ground already and Mother Nature was fixing to dump some more real soon. Therefore, no one really expected to see Wally for a while. And to see him appear upon the scene in such a wild state, made the local pub-goers look at him and shake their heads.

"Old Wally musta got inta sum bad whiskey," Luke Thomas told Harry Parvis. "Either thet or he's took ta makin' his own!"

"Ah dunt know fer sure 'bout thet. But Ah'd shore say thet sumthin' musta scared tha begammers outta him," Harry remarked. "Do ya unnerstain' what he's talkin' 'bout?"

"I ain't got tha foggiest notion. Sumthing 'bout apes iz all Ah can make out," Luke advised.

"Maybe Ah kin git him ta cum over here and try ta make sum sense outta him," Harry said.

He got up from the table and walked over to where Wally was standing, bug-eyed and throwing his arms in wild gestures. Harry put his hand on Wally's shoulder and Wally jumped, throwing Harry's hand into the air.

"Aww, God, Harry, Ah thought 'twas wun uv them apes!!" Wally yelled.

"Whet er ya talkin' 'bout— apes?" Harry asked. "Why don'tcha cum on over ta our table an' tell Luke and me about it, hokay?"

He took Wally's arm and steered him over to the table. He told the barkeep to bring another round and to bring Wally a big, tall one. After they were seated and Wally had had a good sized slug of whiskey, he licked his lips and began his tale.

"Ya knows thet Ah lives a few miles out west of heer. Wahl, ya know hows tha wither's bin tha last few days—all thet snow. Ah jist bin cleanin' mah rifle an' things like thet. Kinda jist rattlin' round in mah cabin. Wahl, sir, tha uther afternoon after it'd quit its snowin', Ah wuz lookin' out tha winder towards tha edge uv tha woods. Taking' in the view—and Ah see sumthin' moving' off there ta tha left. Fust, Ah jist caught it outta tha corner of mah eye. Whin Ah looked d'rectly at it, it wuz a-makin' its way into tha woods. It wuz lookin' back over its shoulder at me!!"

Wally took another big belt of his whiskey and continued with his tale.

"Never seen nuthin' round here tha likes of it before! It weren't more than fifteen yards away whin Ah fust seen it. Wuz standin' up on its hind legs and walkin' jest like a man. But it wuz taller than most min Ah've saw. Prob'ly close ter eight feet high! And covered with black lookin' hair. If this here wuz tha jungle, Ah'd say 'twere un ape! Shore looked a lot like wun!"

Wally paused for a breath and took another drink out of his glass, emptying it.

"Barkeep! Give Wally 'nuther drink," yelled Harry.

"Thankee," Wally said, as the barkeep put the drink down in front of him. "Now, whur wuz Ah?"

"Ya wuz sayin' this here thing ya saw looked like an ape," Luke answered.

"Oh, yah, yah. Wahl, Ah shore wooda gotten my gun and taken out after it, but Ah hadn't gotten it back t'gether yit."

"Jest seein' thet thing the uther day skeered ya 'nuff ta come runnin' in hyar taday?" Luke asked.

"No! No! Ah done seen it agin. An' sum uthers, too!"

"Whin were thet?" Harry asked.

"Late yis'day afternoon whin Ah fust saw um agin. They wuz in 'bout the same place, maybe a little ter tha west. But pert near where Ah saw tha wun that uther day."

"How minny wuz thur?" Luke asked, frowning.

"Four or five. Maybe more. Ah ain't quite shore. Anyways, Ah grabbed mah gun, opened tha door and fired. Ah guesses Ah musta wounded wun uv 'em and they all took off. Ah put on mah coat and

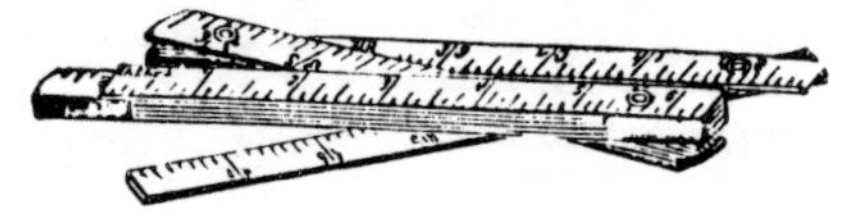

went down whur they'd bin. Wahl, Ah found some blood in tha snow. But those footprints!!! 'Tweren't nuthin' like Ah'd dun seen in mah life afore! Each wun wuz 'bout a foot-and-half long and 'bout eight

or nine inches wide. Only had four toes, so's Ah know culdn't a-bin no bar, 'cause they've got five toes! Also, whutever they wuz, had long toes with short claws. Tha ball uv tha foot made a deep mark inna snow, not like a man. Ya know, a man's heel makes a deeper mark than tha ball of hiz foot, 'cause he steps on his heel fust."

"Wuz it tha paw-prints thet skeered ya, Wally?" Luke asked.

"No, sir, 'tweren't!! Them dad-burned ape-men cum back jist afore dark lass 'snight!"

Wally again stopped his story to slake his thirst and then continued.

"Ah'd finished eatin' an' wuz havin' a coupla drinks when Ah heerd this here noise, like sumwin hittin' tha house. Wahl, Ah tells ya—Ah blew out thet kerosene lamp real fast! Then Ah stood off ter tha side so's Ah culd see 'em up close. They wuz TALL! And covered with short, dark hair. Their heads wuz higher at tha back than at tha front. Their noses wuz flat and their lips was stuck out. The ears looked more like ours, but their eyes wuz small and beady—like a bear's eyes! Their necks wuz short and thicker then a man's."

Wally's hands were shaking as he took another drink, and he slooshed part of it on his chin, which he wiped off with the back of his hand.

"Whet wuz they doin'?" Harry asked.

"Ah think they wuz tryin' ta git at me fer shootin' wun uv 'em," Wally answered.

"Wuzn't ya skeered ta jist stand there lookin' at 'em?" Luke asked.

"Shore, Ah wuz," Wally exclaimed. "Fact is, Ah think ah had un accident in mah britches right then and there. Ah ain't shore jest when it happened, as things got worse!"

"Whet happened next, Wally?" Harry asked.

"Wahl, one or more of 'em knocked uh heavy strip uh wood outta betwixt two logs. But—Ah dunt know wether ya know it or not—Ah built thet cabin ta withstand these here cold Minniesota winters. So, them things din't git in ta me!!"

He again interrupted his story to wet his whistle. The whiskey had helped to steady his nerves, as his hands no longer shook. Harry and Luke glanced at each other with questioning looks on their faces. Wally sounded like he was telling the truth - at least believed what he was telling them was the truth.

"Did they go away then?" Harry asked.

"Oh, no, not fer quite awhile. Them thar ape-men started in a-throwin' sumthin' at mah cabin - at least, thet's whet it sounded like. Ah don't know whet, but Ah shore knows they wuz makin' a whole lotta noise. Ah'd braced tha door with the

table when they fust cum back. But Ah culd heer 'em up on tha roof, walkin' around an' then slidin' off!! They wuz batterin' the walls sumthin' fierce! Ah fired mah gun through the walls an' tha roof, but it dint make 'em go 'way. Finally, Ah jest grabb-ed mah jug and set down at tha table. Tha more noise they made, tha more Ah drank. Purty quick, tha noise stopped. Ah dunt know whether it 'twere 'cause Ah fell asleep or they went away. All Ah knows iz thet whin Ah woke up 'round daylight, they wuz gone!"

Wally's glass was empty by now and he looked at his two table partners.

"Wuld ya like ter go up ta mah cabin and see?" he asked.

Harry looked at Luke. Luke nodded and the three men got up from the table.

"We kin take mah buckboard," Luke said. "Ah

think Old Bessie kin make it through this snow. We'd shore git there faster then if we wuz walkin'."

Old Bessie had a bit of a rough go of it, but she made it - although it took the better part of two hours.

The three men got down out of the buckboard and Wally took them on a tour of where the ape-men had been. The snow was tromped on as though quite a few animals or men had been in the area. Also, the snow on the roof had been tracked around in. But since it had turned a little warmer that day, the snow had melted so that none of the footprints were clear enough to see what had made them.

Could it have been that some of the local boys were playing pranks on Old Wally? And that in his drunken state, he imagined them to be ape-men? Could it have been that in a drunken nightmare, Wally himself had gone out there and made all those tracks?

Or could it have been, in fact, what the Salish Indians call Sasquatch—"Wild man of the woods"?

CHAPTER FIFTEEN

A MODERN DAY ROBIN HOOD?

fter the First National Bank job in Northfield, Minnesota, the James gang headed back to Missouri. Before they reached the Iowa border, the gang stopped at a widow's house for a meal.

While eating and talking, the widow mentioned to Jesse that she was going to lose her farm that day. She then broke down and told him that she just didn't have the money to pay the mortgage.

"How much would it take to pay it off?" Jesse inquired.

"Eight hundred dollars. But it might as well be eight thousand. I've sold off everything I could, but I just cain't raise that kinda money," she replied.

Jesse stood up and reached into his pocket, pulling out a roll of bills. He counted out eight hundred dollars and gave it to the widow. This poor lady stood, money in hand, with a shocked look in her eyes and her mouth dropped open. She had trouble recovering her voice enough to thank Jesse for his kindness. In her excitement, she let some pancakes burn on the top of the stove - but no one cared.

"But there's one thing I wantcha ta do," Jesse told her.

"What's that?" she asked, clutching the bills to her bossom.

"The banker's comin' out here shortly to git his money, right?"

"Yes. He said he'd be here sometime before noon."

"Well, when he gits here and you give him the money, make sure ya git a paid receipt.

"Yessir, I'll do that."

"Well, ma'm, I s'pose we'd better git goin'. We got a long ride ahead of us.

The widow looked down at her calloused hands, callouses she'd gotten trying to earn just enough to get by. She then looked at the money - more than she'd ever seen at one time in her life! She didn't even stop to think that it might be illgotten!

After the gang left the widow's house, they rode a short ways down the road to where there was a thicket of trees on either side. They tied up their horses and then hid themselves.

A little before noon they saw a tall, thin man riding toward the widow's farm. Deciding that it must be the banker on his way to collect his money, the gang let him go about his business. They just stayed in hiding and waited. Even though they knew they were being hunted, Jesse felt that they could spare the time to help a poor widow woman.

About fifteen minutes later, the gang saw the man coming back. They waited until he was almost even with them and then sprang out of the thicket. While one held the horse's reins, two of them relieved the banker of his money—much to his dismay!! Slapping the horse on the rear, the gang sent the banker on his way - minus Jesse's $800!

The widow had her farm paid for. Jesse had his money back. But of course, not everyone basked in the sunshine that day!

CHAPTER SIXTEEN

OLD ABE, THE CHEERLEADER

n today's world of sports, the teams all have cheerleaders to root them on to victory. They serve to get the guys' blood all revved up so that their main thought is to get out there and win!

Back during the Civil War, one regiment of Union soldiers camped near Eau Claire, Wisconsin, had themselves an eagle, "Old Abe", that did the same thing. But wait, I'm getting ahead of my story.

It seems that back in 1861, some Indians were down along the Flambeau River to gather sap for maple syrup one spring day. They saw this young eaglet, and since its mama wasn't around, the Indians captured the little bird.

On the way back to their village, they passed the McCann house. The children were playing out in the yard. They weren't afraid of the Indians because the kids knew that the men were of a friendly tribe. Spotting the young eaglet, the McCann youngsters wanted it for a pet.

"Kin we have it, Daddy, huh? Kin we?" they all asked at the same time.

"Would ya trade it fer a sack of corn?" Mr. McCann asked the Indians.

The Indian agreed and the trade was made. The whole family learned to love the eaglet. But as small things have a habit of doing, the young bird soon got too big to keep.

One day, Mr. McCann gathered his children around him.

"Now, ya all know that the eagle has gotten too big fer us to keep, don'tcha?"

The children tearfully agreed. So, Mr. McCann sold the eagle to the Eighth Wisconsin Infantry for five dollars to be their mascot. They named him "Old Abe".

"Old Abe" was a proud bird! He sat there chained to his perch with his head held high. Young men of the surrounding countryside heard of him, and thereby "Old Abe" did his part to attract many new recruits for the Eau Claire Eagles.

This majestic bird went with the troops when they went south into battle. When the fighting started and the cannons thundered and shells burst, "Old Abe" went into his "cheerleader" routine. Spreading his wings, he would shrill forth his screams of delight and defiance. Ohhh! He was a great morale booster!

In fact, he was so good at it that a Confederate general once said of "Old Abe" that he'd much rather capture the eagle than a whole regiment of men!

CHAPTER SEVENTEEN

SPIRIT ROCK

 orth of Keshena, Wisconsin, in Menominee County, stands the famous "Spirit Rock". Legend has it that one night, many moons ago, a Menominee Indian had a dream. In it, Manabush, grandson of Ko-Ko-Mas-Say-Sa, of Medicine, appeared to the man. Manabush invited him to visit the god.

After awaking the Indian took seven of his friends and called on Manabush. Most of the men asked to be made successful hunters. But one of the band had to be different. He asked the god for eternal life. This angered Manabush! He seized the warrior by the shoulders and thrust him into the ground, saying, "You shall be a stone, thus you will be everlasting!"

The Menominee say that at night, kindly spirits come to lay tobacco at the rock. They also say that if you look closely enough, you can see the white veils among the trees.

(127)

The legend claims that when the rock finally
crumbles away, the race will become extinct!

CHAPTER EIGHTEEN

THE MA BARKER/
ALVIN KARPIS GANG

a Barker was a fearsome gun moll back in the 1930's. She and her four homicidal sons joined up with the Alvin Karpis gang. Putting their collective heads together, they decided to do some kidnapping for profit.

They pulled off one job with complete success, that of kidnapping the brewer, William Hamm, Jr. and collected the healthy sum of $100,000 for his safe return.

Since the Hamm kidnapping and ransoming had been so easy, they thought they should do something for an encore. The gang choose as their next victim the president of a St. Paul bank - one Edward Brenner. Only this time, the price tag should be much higher, more in the range of $200,000!

The murderous matriarch of the gang planned all the details. Mr. Brenner was captured just as Ma instructed. Ransom notes were sent. The hoods demanded that the ransom money - in five and ten dollar bills - be left at a specified rendezvous on the outskirts of Rochester. In response to their demand, the money was left there and Edward Brenner was released on a lonely Minnesota road.

The fearsome moll now issued orders as to how the $200,000 should be divided up. Knowing that the money wasn't exactly a present from the FBI, she figured the bills were more than likely marked.

Ma wasn't one to handle money lightly. So, she divided the $200,000 into two packets, one of which was turned over to one of the gang members. He was to head for Cuba to dispose of this hot currency to a "fence", who would, in turn, convert the marked money into bills which were more spendable.

The other packet was put into a metal cash box, which was then wrapped in canvas. Ma, her son, Fred, and two other gang members then drove 19 miles southeast of Rochester to a gravel road in the country. Getting out of the car, Ma and Fred climbed over a ditch and dug a hole along a farmer's fence line. Into the hole, Ma put the kid-nap cash.

"Safer than a bank," she laughingly told Fred. But all he could do was gripe about having to dig the hole. He wasn't used to doing such menial labor!

As Ma had said, the money was safe all right! But it seems that Ma and Fred weren't. They left Minnesota and went to their Florida hideout. Before the gang member that went to Cuba could get back with cash in hand, Ma and Fred were killed in a shoot-out with the FBI. The rest of the gang divided up the money from the Cuba "fence", but only had a vague idea as to where Ma had buried the cash box.

So, sometime if you're driving down Hwy. 12 in Minnesota, between Rochester and Chatfield, you might be reminded that somewhere out there is a "post-hole bank". It's under one of only several thousand fence posts, or where there used to be fence posts, in that area.

CHAPTER NINETEEN

PAT VARLEY, MARSHAL

umberland lies on what was formerly an island in a lake in Barron County in northern Wisconsin. Filled ground now connects it with the mainland.

The town is a member of the notorious quartette which were the toughest lumber camps in Wisconsin. They used to say, "Cumberland, Hurley, Hayward, and Hell. The first three are tougher than the last!!"

In 1884, there were 24 saloons to serve a few hundred inhabitants of Cumberland.

It was during that time that some of the more sober and conservative citizens of Cumberland hired Pat Varley, an outsider as marshal. This was at the unheard of salary of $100 a month! Varley, who wanted himself known in town, made a formal call on every saloon. He introduced himself as the new marshal and warned all the boys - including those in the backroom, to behave themselves!

At dusk that evening, while making his rounds, he passed a lumberyard. A dozen men led by saloonkeeper Nels Paulson, leaped upon him and dragged him in between two huge stacks of lumber. The men took off their coats and began to roll up their sleeves.

Varley looked Paulson in the eye, saying, "You know, Paulson, you look like a real man to me. You shouldn't be a party to a raw deal like this and you know it."

Paulson didn't answer, just sneered at the new marshal and continued rolling up his sleeves.

"Well, I'll tell you this, Paulson, You'd better kill me while you're at it. Because I'm not the kind of man you can drive out of town. And another thing, each and everyone of you is going to have to deal with me afterwards. You can be sure of that!!"

Paulson kept looking at Varley in the same way. Apparently, he didn't really care if the boys DID kill Varley!

The marshal continued try-ing to talk Paulson out of go-ing through with his plan.

"I'll bargain with you, Paulson," Varley said. "We'll settle it just between you and me in a fair fight. If by chance you lick me, I'll get out of town. BUT!!! IF I LICK YOU, then I'll be staying on as marshal!"

Paulson thought a moment and then accepted the challenge.

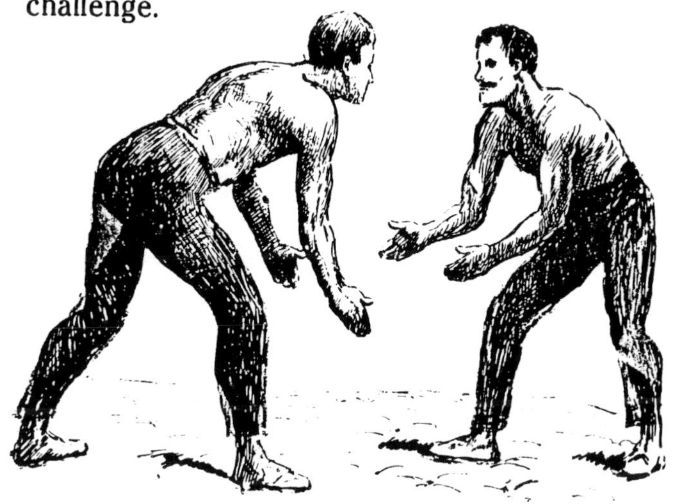

Both men stripped to the waist. They decided there would be no holds barred. The pair — evenly matched — fought for 45 minutes.

Finally, Paulson, showing signs of exhaustion, made a wrong move and Varley won.

For a number of years afterward, Pat Varley, as marshal of Cumberland, was able to maintain some sort of law and order among his unruly flock!

CHAPTER TWENTY

MAIDEN ROCK

aiden Rock consists of a rocky bluff towering four hundred feet above the Mississippi River in Pierce County, Wisconsin. There is a romantic legend behind its name.

It seems that years and years ago, when the white man had yet to come into this land, there lived a young and beautiful Lakota maiden. She was in love with a young Lakota brave. They wanted to marry, but her family insisted that he was not the man for her. They had another picked out for her, a man whom she despised.

The Indian maiden was able to avoid the marriage for nearly a year, hoping that she would be able to marry her true love. But the young brave was sent away from the village. Then she was forced to marry the man her family has chosen.

It was evening and the maiden had been married

less than an hour when she was missed from the lodge. Everyone looked for her, but could not find her in the darkness.

The next morning, the whole tribe was upset. The young maiden had not come back! All the men went looking for her. When they came to the edge of the bluff, they stood silently, looking at the bottom! There, in a heap, lay the body of the young Lakota maiden where she had thrown herself!

CHAPTER TWENTY-ONE

DILLINGER AND THE G-MEN

 estled in the pines of the north woods of Wisconsin, sat an isolated roadhouse known as "Little Bohemia". It was about 8 miles southeast of Mercer—in Iron County. This pub was the scene of a shootout between the gangster, John Dillinger and the G-men.

In the afternoon of April 20, 1934, the owner of the pub looked out the window as three cars pulled up out front. He took a hurried swipe at the bar with his towel. The place was empty and he welcomed the unexpected business.

As the door opened for the group, he looked into the cold gray eyes of a small man. He and his friends were going to stay for a while, the owner was informed. Only then did the bartender realize that he was talking to John Dillinger and that his "friends" were members of his gang, including "Baby Face" Nelson, and their molls.

The owner just shook his head in bewilderment, licked his dry lips and blurted out, "W-w-what'll ya have, folks?"

One of the gang members opened up a suitcase and took out a tommy-gun. The others stepped up to the bar and began a weekend of drinking. They played the gambling machines that lined the wall. When they got tired of this, the gang sang bawdy songs.

Then Dillinger sent the man with the machine gun up to the roof in case there was any unexpected trouble. One of the gang stayed with the owner of the pub day and night for the next three days.

By way of the grapevine, the FBI found out that Dillinger and his gang had taken over the roadhouse. They made immediate plans to capture them. The G-men arrived by plane on Sunday afternoon. They took their assigned places around the roadhouse, knowing that they could not attack before nightfall.

Meanwhile, as the G-men waited and watched from their hiding places, three men came out of the tavern. These men, CCC workers, went to their car parked nearby. They got in and headed toward the highway. The Federal men thought they were part of the Dillinger mob and opened fire.

This alerted Dillinger inside the roadhouse, and it was only moments before the air between the FBI and the bad guys was filled with lead. The acrid odor of gunsmoke burned their noses and throats. The flying glass from the shot-up bottles of liquor rained down upon the fair damsels cowering behind the bar. Both sides luckily escaped the other's bullets.

While the G-men were trying to find out who was in the car, the gangsters crawled out the back window and into the woods to safety!

The FBI had no way of knowing that the mob had
fled. The next morning at dawn, they blasted the
tavern with machine guns and tear-gas bombs. The
heavy boot that smashed the door down revealed
only the three women hiding behind the bar. The
male members of the most vicious mob in the an-
nals of modern crime had eluded the lawmen!

CHAPTER TWENTY-TWO

THE WITCHER-WOMAN

ife was not easy for anyone during the Great Depression of 1893. Well-educated men had to take menial jobs in order to feed their families. Some even sold apples on street corners. Others took to the rails, thinking his fortune may lay beyond the horizon. Many never returned.

Daniel Monihan's family had come to this country a while before the turn of the century. His father had money, and through wise investments accumulated a small fortune. Then came the depression of 1893. The family lost everything. Daniel's father boarded a freight one day, not having the price of a ticket. He wanted to see if California had something to offer. His family never heard from him again.

Daniel had been in his last year of college at the time, but had to quit before graduation. He was studying to be a teacher. Knowing the nature of people, there would always be kids. But things didn't work out that way.

Daniel took any odd-job he could find to keep a roof over his and his mother's heads. But there just wasn't enough money to go around. Many days Daniel was lucky to have even one meal to put into his rumbling stomach.
The house was never warm enough. His mother being in delicate health, came down with pneumonia. The doctor said that was the cause of her death. But Daniel knew better. He knew her death had more to do with a broken will and a broken heart than it did pneumonia.

The next spring, Daniel hopped a freight and made his way to Minnesota. He thought he might find a job in a logging camp around Oshkosh or someplace. But the depression had hurt the lumber business, too, and so he went on foot in search of work.

Foot-weary and weak from hunger, Daniel plopped down on a bench in front of the general store. He decided he couldn't make it any further. If he was going to die, this was as good a place as any! He leaned his head back against the wall of the store and closed his eyes.

A hand on his shoulder awoke him with a start!

"Well, young feller," said a kindly, bewhiskered man. "Thought ya might do with a bite ta eat. Am I wrong?"

"No! You're right—I could!"

"Come on inta tha store and we'll see what we kin find."

The two men made their way to the back of the store. In back of some empty cases was a table and two chairs.

"I wuz just gonna fix mahself a sandwich and thought ya might be able ta use one, too," the store owner told Daniel.

"I'm mighty grateful, mister," Daniel said.

The grocer made Daniel a generous sandwich, and then took a quart of milk out of the icebox. Setting it down in front of Daniel, he then fixed himself a sandwich.

(145)

"Wahtcha doing' in these parts, son?"

Daniel told him his sad tale. When the store owner found out that Daniel had a college education - almost - he sat, chewing on a thumbnail, deep in thought for a few minutes.

"I got an ideer. Some of these people around could do with a good dose of learnin'. There ain't bin a schoolhouse here fer years. I got a empty room in back that might do, if we made some benches . . . Got some rough planks out back. Whatcha say? Care to give it a try?"

"Sounds great! But what would I do for a place to live and something to eat?" Daniel asked.

"As far as a place to live - there's an empty house at tha edge of town. Nobody's lived in it since Jed Carson was killed there a couple of years back. Some say it's haunted. Ya skeered a spooks?"

"No. . .no, but I still need a job that pays money in order to eat, you know."

"Well, son, I'll tell ya what. Let's jest say that the depression didn't hurt me like some folks. So, maybe I kin afford ta feed ya - for awhile, at least," the owner told Daniel.

"But what would you be getting out of all this?"

"Jest the feelin' that maybe I wuz doin' my part ta help out tha people 'round here. That's all, son, but it's enough."

"How would you go about getting the children in here for school?" Daniel asked.

"I'd put uppa sign outside and in the store. At least, that'd be uh start. Then we'd go frum there. But I'm thinkin' it's more than just kids that need to learn their ABC's. Their parents could use it, too, but I ain't sure they'd come."

"Well, I guess we'll just have to wait and see, won't we? Oh, by the way. What'll we use for school supplies?"

"Just what all would ya need?"

"A blackboard, chalk, tablets, pencils. Books, too, if we could get them."

"After we git them benches built and all sech, I'll see what I kin cum up with. Okay?"

"You know, mister, I don't even know your name.

(147)

Yet you've come up with more help for me then anyone else besides my family," Daniel told the store owner.

"I'm Sherm Godfrey, boy. But I don't know yer name, either," Sherm said, smiling.

"Oh! Of course you don't! I'm sorry! It's Daniel— Daniel Monihan."

"Okay, Daniel, we've got that out of the way. Now . . . you need some rest. I've got a cot in the back room. Why not take a nap and we'll talk some more later. Tomorrow's another day. Soon enough to get started on our schoolroom."

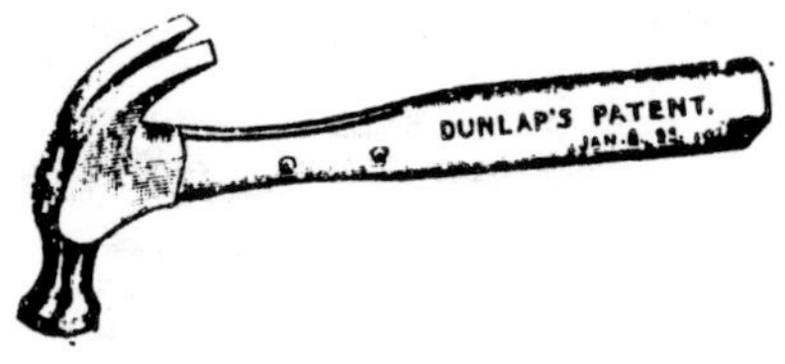

The next day, Daniel started getting the benches built. Though crude, they served the purpose. Sherm, when he had the chance, went through some of his stuff in a storage room. He found a few old school books, a pull-down map, and a high wooden stool. A few days later, Sherm went to a bigger town a few miles away, in his wagon. He got the school supplies that Daniel had requested, including, the black-boards and chalk.

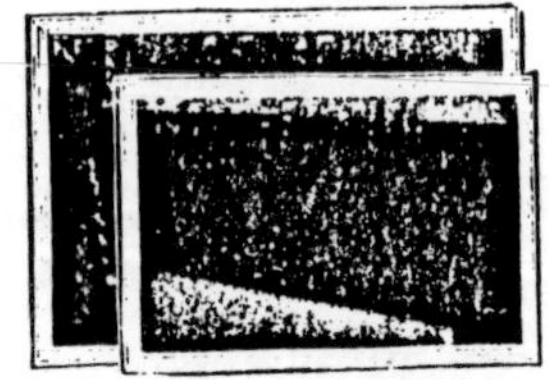

When the schoolroom was ready for "business", the signs were tacked up. They invited everybody - young and old alike - to come and "git educated". At first, there were a few young people that started coming on a regular basis. Then a few older persons came. Daniel knew that it took a lot of guts on their part and he admired them for it.

One day Sherm handed Daniel a note when he walked in.

"What's this?" Daniel asked.

"Someone was interested in gettin' some schoolin'. She left this here note to give to ya. Don't know if you'd be interested or not, though."

"Why shouldn't I be interested?" Daniel asked.

"Read the note first," Sherm advised him.

Daniel opened the note and read:

> "Deer sur. They saide that you was holdin' school in the back room. My mama done teached me sum. Butt ah wood like to larn more. Pleez cum out ta sea me soon. Mr. Godfree kin tell ya whar ah lives.
>
> Thankee,
> Annabelle Winters"

Daniel folded the note and put it in his pocket. He turned to Sherm, his eyebrows knitted together in a frown.

"Why didn't you think I'd be delighted? From the looks of this note, she's had SOME education. I think it's great, don't you?"

Sherm looked out the window for a couple of minutes before he answered.

"I guess it's great if ya think so. I jest don't know."

"What is it, Sherm?"

"It's her!"

"What about her?"

"Well . . . all right, I'll jist come right out an' tell ya. She's a witcher woman, Daniel!"

"She casts spells on people an' things like thet," Sherm replied.

"Oh, come on, Sherm! You surely don't believe in that stuff, do you?"

"I guess ah does—at least, some of it."

"Well, I don't! Where does she live, Sherm?"

"You ain't really goin' out there, are ya?"

"If you'll tell me where! There's no school today. And if you'd let me use your horse and wagon, I'd like to go calling on this Annabelle Winters."

"Yaw, I'll let ya use 'em. But ah hopes ta God nuthin' happens!"

"Now, Sherm. Nothing to going to happen."

Daniel and Sherm went out to the barn behind the store. Sherm hitched his horse to the wagon. Daniel climbed up and Sherm gave him directions. As Daniel pulled away, Sherm made the sign of the cross after him.

When Daniel arrived at Annabelle's house, he tied
the horse to the fence and knocked on the cabin
door. Annabelle promptly opened the door. Daniel
introduced himself and she invited him in.

He noticed that even though sunshine was pour-
ing in through the windows, there were a number
of candles burning on the mantle of the fireplace
and on the table. Annabelle noticed and smiled.

"They's ta keep the bad spirits away," she told him.

"Oh. What kind of spirits are we talking about, Miss
Winters?"

"Oh, there's all kinds," she said, smiling.

Daniel noticed that she was a very attractive
woman. He wondered why no man had made her
his wife long ago. She looked like a great catch!

(152)

Before he left Annabelle's house that day, they made arrangements for Daniel to come out there of an evening to do some private tutoring. He was quite smitten with his Annabelle Winters.

When he returned the horse and wagon to Sherm, they had a good talk.

"Well, Daniel. How'd it go?"

"Fine. Just fine, Sherm."

"How'd ja like 'er?"

"I think she's a very nice and beautiful woman, Sherm. She's also smart. I think she'll be a delight to teach."

"But she's evil, Daniel!! She makes people get sick and die! She can make a cow's milk go sour! Some

have seen her riding a broom at night! She also makes bad weather!"

"Sherm! Sherm! Come on! You can't really believe that kind of stuff about her, can you?!"

(153)

"She already done cast a spell over ya, Daniel, and ya don't even know it!"

Daniel went to his cabin a little downcast. That was the closest to an argument he'd had with Sherm. But he'd been taken quite aback by the "witcher woman", he agreed. Oh, she wasn't one of the girls he was used to back east, but he was sure she was a gem in the rough, and he was planning on doing the polishing!!

Sherm continued to loan his horse and wagon to Daniel, though he wasn't thrilled about his using it to go to Annabelle's.

Daniel went to her house to teach her for several weeks. Then came the rainy season. He couldn't make it out there for several days. The creek was bank full close to Annabelle's house. Daniel began to worry that it might flood her place. He decided to go out that way and check on her.

He put on a slicker and walked up to Sherm's store. By the time he got there, his pants were sopping wet up to his knees and his shoes and socks were soaked.

"What in God's name eer ya doin' out on a day like this, Daniel?" Sherm asked him.

"Can I borrow your horse to go check on Annabelle?"

"You've gotta be outen yer mind ta even think 'bout going' in all this rain!! Look atcha! Yer soakin' wet now!"

"Please, Sherm. I'm worried about the creek flooding her place!"

Though he hated to have his horse out in the downpour, he let Daniel borrow it.

The poor animal had a rough go of it, trying to get through all the thick mud on the road. Finally, looking like a pair of drowned rats, Daniel and the horse made it to Annabelle's cabin. But she did not answer his knock on the door. It was unlocked and he went in. Daniel could not find Annabelle and all of the candles had burned out.

Running around the cabin, Daniel kept calling her name. He realized that he had fallen in love with her and fretted that something might have happened! Daniel went to the creek which was out of its banks and rushing swiftly toward the river.

Daniel ran along the shore, shouting Annabelle's name. He ran until he was gasping for breath. He stopped and looked around. Spotting a fallen tree, he went over to it. There, amongst its branches that were in the creek, was Annabelle. Her clothes

had caught on it and the water was washing over
her still body in waves!

That rushing water mocked those voices who had
spoken of Annabelle being anything other than a
beautiful woman.

He took off his hat and put it over his heart. Bow-
ing his head, Daniel said a little prayer for the
"witcher woman"—and his lost love!!

EPILOGUE

So, the witcher woman proved to nothing more, and nothing less, than a beautiful woman . . . a woman for whom love came too late.

And, then there was Pat Varely who had to wrestle fight the town bully in order to keep his job . . . and the Civil War's only feathered cheerleader.

Were Wally Ferguson's ape-men real or did they materalize out of the fumes of a whiskey bottle?

It's too bad about Grandpa Harry shootin' the preacher that way, and how Betsy Callahan took a sawdust bath, but that's the way thing went in the Lake Country years ago.

Need A Gift?

For

- **Shower** • **Birthday** • **Mother's Day** •
  • **Anniversary** • **Christmas** •

Turn Page for Order Form
(Order Now While Supply Lasts!)

To Order Copies Of

Gun Shootin' Girl Chasin' Whiskey Drinkin' Tales Out of the Land of the Lakes

Please send me _______ copies of **Gun Shootin' Girl Chasin' Whiskey Drinkin' Tales Out of the Land of the Lakes** at $9.95 each. (Make checks payable to **QUIXOTE PRESS.**)

Name _______________________________________

Street ______________________________________

City _______________ State ______ Zip ______

Send Orders To:
Quixote Press
R.R. #4, Box 33B • Blvd. Station
Sioux City, Iowa 51109

- -

To Order Copies Of

Gun Shootin' Girl Chasin' Whiskey Drinkin' Tales Out of the Land of the Lakes

Please send me _______ copies of **Gun Shootin' Girl Chasin' Whiskey Drinkin' Tales Out of the Land of the Lakes** at $9.95 each. (Make checks payable to **QUIXOTE PRESS.**)

Name _______________________________________

Street ______________________________________

City _______________ State ______ Zip ______

Send Orders To:
Quixote Press
R.R. #4, Box 33B • Blvd. Station
Sioux City, Iowa 51109

INDEX

STRANGE FOLKS ALONG THE MISSISSIPPI
by Pat Wallace . . . . .paperback $9.95

THE VANISHING OUTHOUSE OF IOWA
by Bruce Carlson . . . . .paperback $9.95

THE VANISHING OUTHOUSE OF ILLINOIS
by Bruce Carlson . . . . .paperback $9.95

THE VANISHING OUTHOUSE OF MINNESOTA
by Bruce Carlson . . . . .paperback $9.95

THE VANISHING OUTHOUSE OF WISCONSIN
by Bruce Carlson . . . . .paperback $9.95

MISSISSIPPI RIVER COOKIN' BOOK
by Bruce Carlson . . . . .paperback $11.95

IOWA'S ROAD KILL COOKBOOK
by Bruce Carlson . . . . .paperback $7.95

HITCH HIKING THE UPPER MIDWEST
by Bruce Carlson . . . . .paperback $7.95

IOWA, THE LAND BETWEEN THE VOWELS
by Bruce Carlson . . . . .paperback $9.95
(Farm Boy Stories From the Early 1900's)

GHOSTS OF SOUTHWEST MINNESOTA
by Ruth Hein . . . . .paperback $9.95

ME 'N WESLEY
by Bruce Carlson . . . . .paperback $9.95
*(Stories about the homemade toys that farm children made
and played with around the turn of the century.)*

SOUTH DAKOTA ROAD KILL COOKBOOK
by Bruce Carlson . . . . .paperback $7.95

GHOSTS OF THE BLACK HILLS
by Tom Welch . . . . .paperback $9.95

**Some Pretty Tame, But Kinda Funny Stories
About Early DAKOTA LADIES-OF-THE-EVENING**
by Bruce Carlson . . . . .paperback $9.95

**Some Pretty Tame, But Kinda Funny Stories
About Early IOWA LADIES-OF-THE EVENING**
by Bruce Carlson ....paperback $9.95

**Some Pretty Tame, But Kinda Funny Stories
About Early ILLINOIS LADIES-OF-THE-EVENING**
by Bruce Carlson ....paperback $9.95

**Some Pretty Tame, But Kinda Funny Stories
About Early MINNESOTA
LADIES-OF-THE-EVENING**
by Bruce Carlson ....paperback $9.95

**Some Pretty Tame, But Kinda Funny Stories
About Early WISCONSIN
LADIES-OF-THE-EVENING**
by Bruce Carlson ....paperback $9.95

**Some Pretty Tame, But Kinda Funny Stories
About Early MISSOURI LADIES-OF-THE-EVENING**
by Bruce Carlson ....paperback $9.95

THE DAKOTA'S VANISHING OUTHOUSE
Bruce Carlson ....paperback $9.95

ILLINOIS' ROAD KILL COOKBOOK
by Bruce Carlson ....paperback $7.95

OLD IOWA HOUSES, YOUNG LOVES
by Bruce Carlson ....paperback $9.95
(Stores about old houses in Iowa and young loves they have known.)

TERROR IN THE BLACK HILLS
Dick Kennedy ....paperback $9.95

IOWA'S EARLY HOME REMEDIES
by various ....paperback $9.95

GHOSTS OF DOOR COUNTY, WISCONSIN
by Geri Rider......................paperback $9.95

THE VANISHING OUTHOUSE OF MISSOURI
by Bruce Carlson ....paperback $9.95

JACK KING vs DETECTIVE MACKENZIE
by N. Bell . . . . paperback $9.95

RIVER SHARKS & SHENANIGANS
(Tales of Riverboat Gambling of Years Ago)
by N. Bell . . . . paperback $9.95

TALES OF HACKETT'S CREEK
(1940's Mississippi River Kids)
by D. Titus . . . . paperback $9.95

LOST & BURIED TREASURE OF THE MISSOURI RIVER
by N. Bell . . . . paperback $9.95

GHOSTS OF THE OZARKS
by Bruce Carlson . . . . paperback $9.95

UNSOLVED MYSTERIES OF THE MISSISSIPPI
by N. Bell . . . . paperback $9.95

TALL TALES OF THE MISSISSIPPI RIVER
by D. Titus . . . . paperback $9.95

TALL TALES OF THE MISSOURI RIVER
by D. Titus . . . . paperback $9.95

MAKIN' DO IN SOUTH DAKOTA
by various . . . . paperback $9.95

TRICKS WE PLAYED IN IOWA
by various . . . . paperback $9.95

CHILDREN OF THE RIVER
by various . . . . paperback $9.95

LET'S GO DOWN TO THE RIVER 'AN . . .
by various . . . . paperback $9.95

EARLY WISCONSIN HOME REMEDIES
by various . . . . paperback $9.95

EARLY MISSOURI HOME REMEDIES
by various . . . . paperback $9.95

MY VERY FIRST . . .
by various . . . . paperback $9.95

101 WAYS FOR IOWANS TO "DO IN THEIR NEIGHBOR'S PESKY DOG WITHOUT GETTING CAUGHT

by Bruce Carlson ....paperback $7.95

SOUTH DAKOTA ROADKILL COOKBOOK

by Bruce Carlson ....paperback $7.95

A FIELD GUIDE TO IOWA'S CRITTERS

by Bruce Carlson ....paperback $7.95

A FIELD GUIDE TO MISSOURI'S CRITTERS

by Bruce Carlson ....paperback $7.95

MISSOURI'S ROADKILL COOKBOOK

by Bruce Carlson ....paperback $7.95

A FIELD GUIDE TO ILLINOIS' CRITTERS

by Bruce Carlson ....paperback $7.95

MINNESOTA'S ROADKILL COOKBOOK

by Bruce Carlson ....paperback $7.95

REVENGE OF THE ROADKILL

by Bruce Carlson ....paperback $7.95

THE MOTORIST'S FIELD GUIDE TO MIDWEST FARM EQUIPMENT

(Misguided Information as only a City Slicker can get it messed up.)
by Bruce Carlson ....paperback $7.95

ILLINOIS EARLY HOME REMEDIES

by various ....paperback $9.95

GUNSHOOTIN', WHISKEY DRINKIN', GIRL CHASIN' TALES OUT OF THE OLD DAKOTA TERRITORY

by Netha Bell ....paperback $9.95

EARLY IOWA SCHOOLS

by C. Johnston ....paperback $9.95

WYOMING'S ROADKILL COOKBOOK

by Bruce Carlson ....paperback $7.95

MONTANA'S ROADKILL COOKBOOK
by B. Carlson . . . . paperback $7.95

DOWNHOME IN NEBRASKA
(Tales of Nebraska Housewife)
by M. Walsh . . . . paperback $9.95

SKUNK RIVER ANTHOLOGY
by Gene "Will" Olson . . . . paperback $9.95

**FUNNER-THINGS-TO-DO-THAN-COOKIN'
 COOKBOOK**
by Louise Lum . . . . paperback $11.95

101 WAYS TO USE A DEAD RIVER FLY
by Bruce Carlson . . . . paperback $7.95

MAKIN' DO IN ILLINOIS
by various authors . . . . paperback $9.95

MISSOURI'S OLD HOUSES, AND NEW LOVES
by Bruce Carlson . . . . paperback $9.95

YOU KNOW YOU'RE IN IOWA WHEN . . .
by Bruce Carlson . . . . paperback $7.95

IOWA - A JOURNEY IN A PROMISED LAND
by Kathy Yoder . . . . paperback $16.95

WISCONSIN'S ROADKILL COOKBOOK
by Bruce Carlson . . . . paperback $7.95

UNDERGROUND MISSOURI
by Bruce Carlson . . . . paperback $9.95

**GUNSHOOTIN', WHISKEY DRINKIN', GIRL
CHASIN' STORIES OUT OF THE OLD
MISSOURI TERRITORY**
by Bruce Carlson . . . . paperback $9.95

**VACANT LOT, SCHOOL YARD & BACK ALLEY
GAMES OF THE MIDWEST YEARS AGO**
by various authors ....paperback $9.95

**HOW SOME OF US ITTY-BITTY FOLKS
HERE IN THE MIDWEST WOULD RUN
A HOUSE IF WE HAD TO**
by various authors ....paperback $7.95

**GUNSHOOTIN', WHISKEY DRINKIN', GIRL
CHASIN' STORIES OUT OF THE LAND
OF THE LAKES**
by Netha Bell ....paperback $9.95